IMAGES
of America

SACRAMENTO

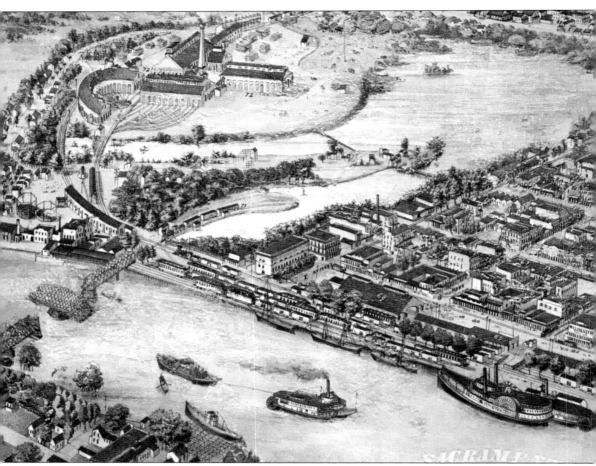

In this detail of Augustus Koch's 1870 aerial map, Sacramento is depicted flourishing after surviving its tumultuous early years. The Central Pacific Railroad shops are at upper left on the banks of Sutter Lake. Sacramento's first railroad bridge spanning the Sacramento River connects the city to Yolo County, while riverboats line the waterfront. Front Street businesses face the river, and I, J, and K Streets lead to the east. (Special Collections of the Sacramento Public Library.)

ON THE COVER: A gaggle of Sacramento Junior College (SJC) students enjoys a carefree evening around 1930. As Sacramento's first institution of higher learning, SJC has served as an educational anchor for over a century. At the time this photograph was taken, SJC was sending many of its graduates to the University of California system, Stanford University, Mills College, Santa Clara University, and several of the state's teaching colleges. (Special Collections of the Sacramento Public Library.)

IMAGES
of America

SACRAMENTO

Special Collections of the
Sacramento Public Library
Foreword by Rivkah K. Sass

ARCADIA
PUBLISHING

Copyright © 2019 by Special Collections of the Sacramento Public Library
ISBN 978-1-4671-0346-6

Published by Arcadia Publishing
Charleston, South Carolina

Printed in the United States of America

Library of Congress Control Number: 2018967185

For all general information, please contact Arcadia Publishing:
Telephone 843-853-2070
Fax 843-853-0044
E-mail sales@arcadiapublishing.com
For customer service and orders:
Toll-Free 1-888-313-2665

Visit us on the Internet at www.arcadiapublishing.com

*For our fallen colleague Amber Clark, a selfless,
loving servant to the people of Sacramento.*

CONTENTS

FOREWORD

One of the joys of serving as library director at the Sacramento Public Library is sharing our community's past through the rich resources of our Sacramento Room and the expertise of staff who are knowledgeable, passionate about history, and eager to share the bounty that represents Sacramento.

Library staff has put together a collection that is part homage, part history, and as you will see as you browse through the content assembled here, a lot of heart. Sacramento represents many things to many people, not always a pretty picture, not always receiving the respect it might deserve, but it is filled with surprises, with hopes, and with a history that is deep, wide, and golden.

While I am not a native, I am a Central Valley girl, born and bred. Sacramento, home to three television stations, was my window to the larger world. As someone who left the area for three decades, it has been a delight to live here while Sacramento is truly coming into its own. Described in Greta Gerwig's *Lady Bird* as the Midwest of California, that has a ring of truth, but so does the description that we are Portland's slightly nerdy cousin.

Whatever your thoughts about California's capital, this book provides insights that will surprise you, and I hope, encourage you to spend more time in the Sacramento Public Library's Sacramento Room.

—Rivkah K. Sass
Library Director/CEO
Sacramento Public Library

ACKNOWLEDGMENTS

We gratefully acknowledge the contributions of the following individuals: Sacramento Public Library director Rivkah K. Sass, Central Library manager Stephanie Manansala, Central Library supervisors Andria McCune and Heather Harrison, library communications analyst Linda Beymer, shelver Kristy Molnar, librarian Gerald Ward, historian Chris Lango, artist Michael Hodgson, photographer Hector Gonzalez, and interns Kristen Utley and Matthew Walker.

We also appreciate the dedicated assistance of our library and archive colleagues in providing many of the images used in this book, in addition to those drawn from the Sacramento Public Library's own collection. They include Rebecca Crowther, Kim Hayden, and Dylan McDonald of the Center for Sacramento History (CSH); Kathleen Correia of the California History Section of the California State Library (CSL); Katie Gilroy of the Board of Regents of the University of California (BRUC); oral historian Bob Tribe (BT); our friends at the Bancroft Library, University of California, Berkeley (BL); the Library of Congress (LOC); and the National Archives and Records Administration (NARA). Unless indicated by any of the aforementioned initials, all images come from the Special Collections of the Sacramento Public Library.

Finally, and perhaps most importantly, we are grateful for the day-to-day contributions of our patrons. It is through their passion and curiosity that we are inspired to be the very best that we can be. Together, we are an irrepressible force for illumination.

INTRODUCTION

"The Heart of California," a slogan penned by Sacramento's Chamber of Commerce in 1911, effectively captures the Capital City's place in history. From the pre–Gold Rush era to the present, Sacramento has not only held a central place geographically but has also exemplified California's spirit and supplied its lifeblood. Sacramento has been constant in its place as California's hub but ever-changing in the face of the industrial innovations and social movements that have transformed the city. Because of its vital role in the region, the history of Sacramento is, in many ways, the history of California and the West.

Since before its founding, Sacramento has been both a point of arrival and embarkation for those new to California. Sutter's Fort, the region's first European settlement, served as the terminus of the California Trail and brought hundreds of settlers from the East to all parts of California and the Oregon Territory in the 1840s. Thousands more came by river from around the world after the 1848 discovery of gold at Coloma. During the Gold Rush, scores of steamers and schooners made their way to the new embarcadero on the Sacramento River, some destined for the mines and others to start businesses supplying them.

In early 1850, Sacramento became the first incorporated city in the state and found its niche in welcoming settlers and facilitating commerce between the mines and the port city of San Francisco. Of the multitudes who arrived in California during the Gold Rush, those who stayed in Sacramento reflected the diversity of gold rushers and built the city with their ingenuity and perseverance. Shaped by their early years spent growing a city in the midst of fires, floods, and epidemics, Sacramentans of the 1850s demonstrated a spirit of vitality, perseverance, and generosity. It was this spirit that state officials cited when selecting Sacramento as the permanent home of the state capitol in 1854.

Sacramento soon became a center for transportation and communication. Pony Express riders finished their 10-day journey in Sacramento, and when the first transcontinental telegraph line was completed in 1861, Sacramento was at the receiving end of its first instantaneous message. The city also became the terminus of the state's first railway in 1855 and, several years later, was chosen as the starting point for construction of the first transcontinental railroad. By the late 1800s, the Southern Pacific Railroad Shops employed thousands, and Sacramento had become the railroading giant's industrial heart. In 1895, the longest transmission powerlines in the United States followed the route of the railroad from the world-class Folsom Powerhouse and electrified the city of Sacramento.

Sacramento became a point of arrival for many thousands from abroad in the late 1800s as the already diverse city developed flourishing populations of Irish, Portuguese, German, Japanese, and Chinese immigrants. Churches, community centers, and social organizations all supported these diverse groups. In the city at large, social groups, like the YMCA and Tuesday Club, and new department stores, like Weinstock, Lubin, and Co. and Hale Bros., brought social activity and cohesion to the city.

At the turn of the 20th century, Sacramento took greater advantage of its Central Valley location. The city's agricultural potential had been recognized since before its founding, although such viability was overshadowed by the Gold Rush. Agricultural production ramped up in the late 1800s, and by the 1910s, Sacramento was growing, canning, and transporting the riches of the most fertile valley in the country. City limits expanded south and east as reclaimed land drew suburban farmers from the east. Sacramento annexed the Oak Park, East Sacramento, and Land Park neighborhoods in 1911, growing the population by nearly 50 percent.

New infrastructure in the early 1900s emphasized Sacramento's place as a transportation center. A network of streetcars brought Sacramentans to new suburban parks on the outskirts of the city, Oak Park, William Land Park, and Curtis Park among them. Sacramentans also embraced their location as a center of the nation's nascent network of highways and became a motoring city, a foretaste of the postwar significance of the interstate highways. Transportation infrastructure projects during this era culminated in the construction of both the Southern Pacific Depot (1927) and Tower Bridge (1935). Out of the economic success driven by agriculture and the railroads, Sacramento built some of its tallest and grandest edifices in the interwar years, including the Elks Tower, California Life Insurance Building, Sacramento High School, and Memorial Auditorium. But the city was not exempt from the struggles of the Great Depression, during which numerous shantytowns sprang up along the American River.

World War II brought economic prosperity and the defense industry into the mix, with the expansion of Mather Field east of town and the activation of McClellan Field to the north, both chosen by way of Sacramento's ideal location within the safety of the Central Valley, positioning as a transportation polestar, and status of boasting one of the best flying climates in the nation. This industry rose to new prominence with the advent of the Cold War, although its greatest impact would be felt in the suburban centers quickly forming outside of the city.

Postwar Sacramentans moved into the suburbs at a rapid rate and built the region's schools, tract homes, and businesses. After residents began to vacate downtown, the heart of Sacramento underwent major transformation with the construction of the interstates and redevelopment. Efforts were made to celebrate Sacramento's Gold Rush history through the rehabilitation of Old Sacramento and the old embarcadero; however, much of the city's hardscrabble West End was torn down in 1960 to make way for a series of redevelopment projects. Central to the state's political power and home to a diverse population, Sacramento also became host to the protest and racial unrest of the civil rights era. As the city entered the 21st century, redevelopment turned to reuse, with movements to celebrate both the urban spirit of Sacramento and its past.

Since the 1910s, Sacramento has taken on many slogans in an effort to capture and market its appeal—the Land of Romance and Recreation, the Camellia Capital of the World, the City of Trees, and the Farm to Fork Capital among them. But regardless of Sacramento's rebranding over the years, the city has demonstrated its enduring place in history as the Heart of California.

—Amanda G. DeWilde

One

THE RIVER CITY RISES
PREHISTORY TO 1869

For thousands of years prior to European arrival, small groups of Nisenan fished and harvested acorns near the Sacramento area's plentiful waterways. The Spanish first arrived in 1808 when explorer Gabriel Moraga ventured inland from San Francisco Bay and navigated a river that he named the Sacramento (or "Blessed Sacrament"). Several expeditions followed over the ensuing years, but John August Sutter, a German-born Swiss immigrant, was the first to lay claim to the land at the confluence of the Sacramento and American Rivers. Sutter obtained the New Helvetia land grant of nearly 50,000 acres from the Mexican government in 1839, and soon after began constructing a trading fort one mile from his landing on the American River. Although hundreds of overland immigrants came to Sutter's Fort in the early 1840s, most continued on to other parts. It was the discovery of gold at Coloma in 1848 that brought thousands to the new embarcadero along the Sacramento River. By 1849, John Sutter Jr. and enterprising businessman Sam Brannan had commissioned a city grid near the embarcadero, and the city of Sacramento was born.

Although Sacramento dates its formal incorporation to March 18, 1850, the city was truly formed out of the fires, floods, epidemics, and upheavals of the decade that followed. The city's first year began with a massive flood, followed by a series of fires that destroyed much of the city, a deadly squatters' riot that resulted in the death of the mayor, and a devastating cholera epidemic that took the lives of hundreds. Where the 1850s was defined by adversity, the 1860s was a decade of construction. Sacramento became the home of the Central Pacific Railroad, built the permanent state capitol, and began raising the city streets to prevent catastrophic flooding. By 1870, Sacramento had established its place as the City of the Plains at the crossroads of mining to the east, agriculture to the north and south, and commerce to the west.

—Amanda G. DeWilde

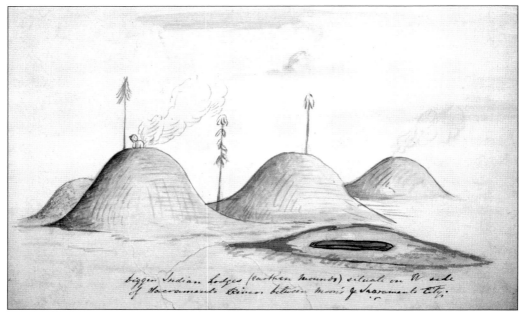

diggin Indian lodges (earthen mounds) situate on W side of Sacramento River, between Moors & Sacramento City.

Nisenan villages were located on or near rivers and other waterways in the Sacramento area. They were composed of dome-shaped dwellings along with a roundhouse or dance house, a small sweathouse, and elevated acorn granaries. Mounded dwellings, like those pictured here, were built with a willow framework and covered by earth or grasses. (BL.)

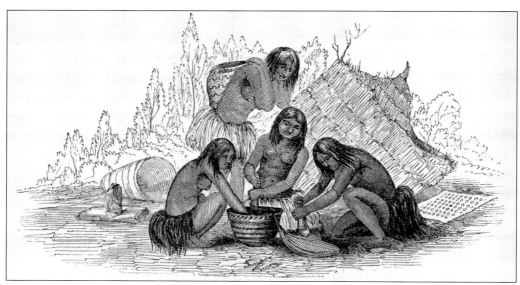

Maidu women pound acorns into meal in this c. 1841 lithograph. The Nisenan pounded acorns using a stone pestle and a mortar made of oak with a burned-out hole. Acorns were a staple of the Nisenan diet, and their cultivation was a key part of their late-summer and early-fall labor.

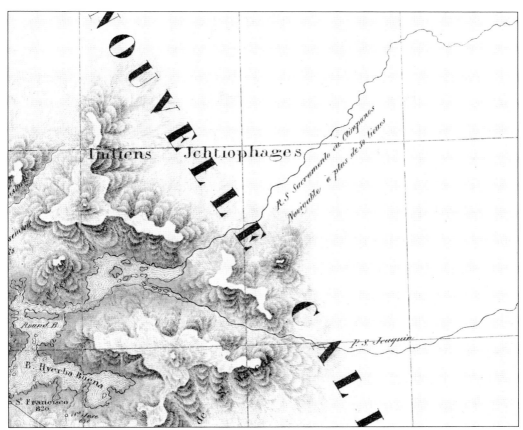

Phillippe Vandermaelen's 1825 map of California is one of the earliest to identify the Sacramento River. Translated, the label reads, "R. S. Sacramento or Timpanogos, Navigable over 50 leagues." Most maps postdating the discovery of the Great Salt Lake in 1824 incorrectly identified the Sacramento River as the Timpanogos River or San Buenaventura, a fabled waterway that was said to run from San Francisco Bay to the Great Salt Lake.

In the late 1820s and 1830s, fur trappers began arriving in the Sacramento Valley, many to search the fabled Buenaventura River. Renowned frontiersman Jedediah Smith was one of the first to explore the valley and was followed by the first Hudson's Bay Company (HBC) trappers in 1829. Malaria, likely carried by infected HBC trappers from Fort Vancouver, wiped out a majority of the native population in the region in 1833.

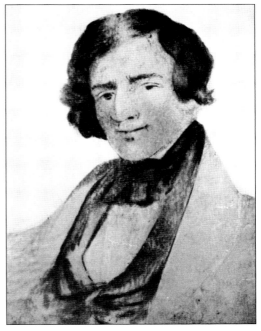

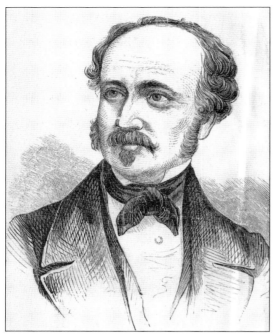

In 1839, John Sutter departed from Monterey equipped with a Mexican passport and power granted by Governor Alvarado to explore and occupy any territory he wished and return within one year to receive a land grant. Accompanied by a party of 14, including eight Kanakas (Hawaiian laborers), Sutter journeyed along the Sacramento River and established the colony of Nueva Helvetia around present-day Sacramento.

This 1848 map of the Sacramento Valley outlines the area's many *ranchos*, or Mexican land grants. Today, the city of Sacramento falls within the historical bounds of John Sutter's Nueva Helvetia grant and Rancho del Paso, granted to Hiram and Eliab Grimes and John Sinclair in 1844. Rancho del Paso covered land north of the Sacramento River, which is today Del Paso Heights and North Sacramento.

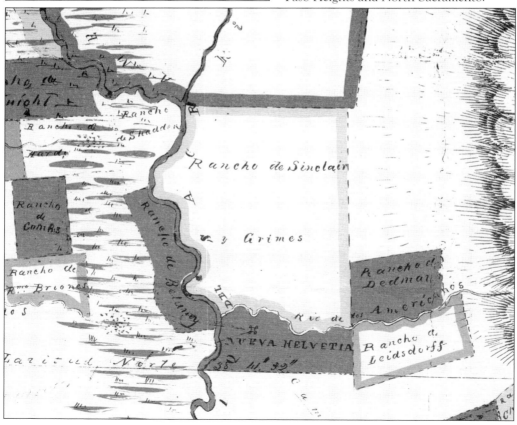

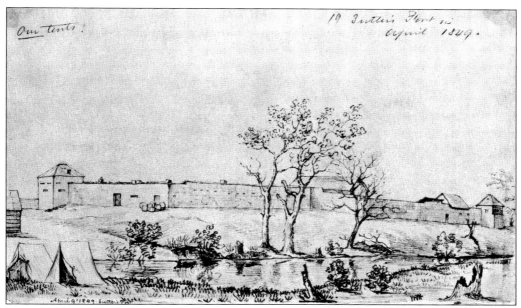

Sutter's Fort, located near present-day L and Twenty-Seventh Streets, began to take shape in 1839 around a 40-foot-long adobe structure. The fort is pictured here in 1849 surrounded by thick protective walls that are 18 feet high and 3 feet thick and equipped with guns and small cannon. At the bottom runs Burns Slough, which originated at the American River in East Sacramento.

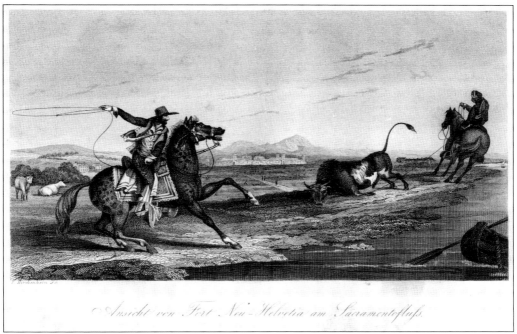

This dramatic depiction of ranching at New Helvetia dates from 1849. John Sutter used Native American labor to engage in numerous moneymaking ventures at Sutter's Fort prior to gold discovery, chief among them being raising cattle and cultivating wheat. Sutter developed a herd of more than 20,000, which provided smoked meat, hides, and tallow.

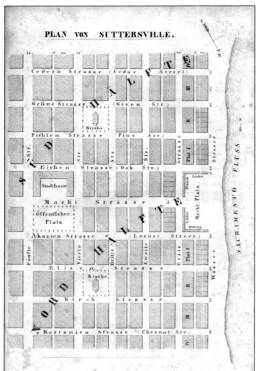

When John Sutter began to plan a city to accommodate the growing needs of the population in and around his fort in 1844, he identified a site three miles south of the confluence on the east bank of the Sacramento River. This map for his self-styled Sutterville was drawn by German guidebook author Bruno Schmolder, who worked with Sutter on plans for colonization.

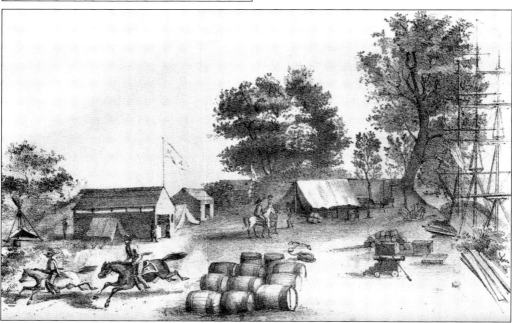

Sutterville began the 1840s with promise, but by the time of this 1849 sketch, it began to lose business and settlers to the bustling new city of Sacramento, which would win out as the commercial center for the mines. After years of decline, Sutterville served as the temporary location for Camp Union, which trained thousands of California volunteers during the Civil War.

Samuel Brannan, pictured here around 1850, was an enterprising businessman who operated the first store in the Sacramento Valley at Sutter's Fort. Upon the discovery of gold at Sutter's Mill in Coloma in 1848, he set his sights on attracting miners to the area. Brannan persuaded John Sutter Jr. to build the city of Sacramento at the confluence of the Sacramento and American Rivers, against Sutter Sr.'s wishes. (CSH.)

This view of the city of Sacramento from the Sacramento River, drawn in 1849 by G.V. Cooper, shows a burgeoning and active young city. Sailing vessels both large and small predominate, though their role would soon slowly diminish. By the early 1850s, Sacramento was served by about two dozen steamers, which transported nearly seven times as much tonnage as sailing ships. (LOC.)

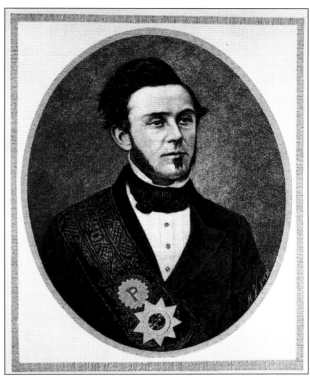

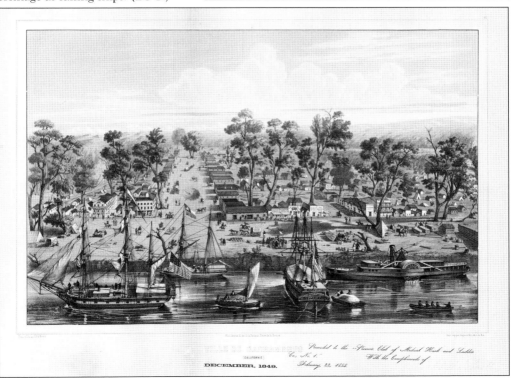

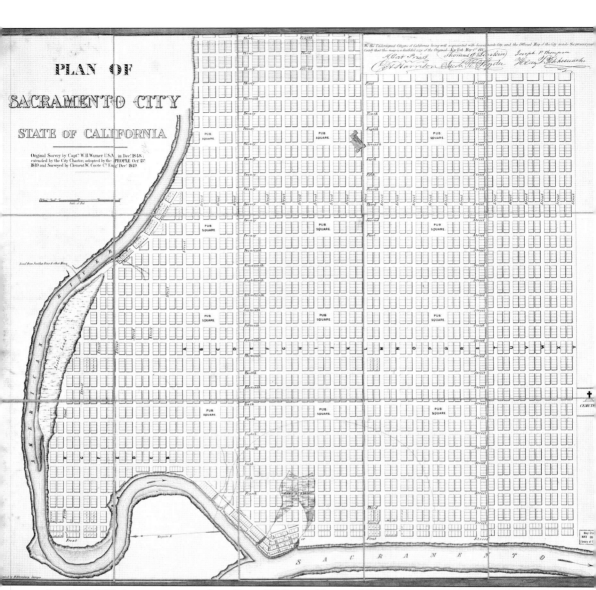

In 1848, US Army cartographer Capt. William Horace Warner was commissioned by John Sutter Jr. to lay out a plan for the prospective city of Sacramento. His map shows a familiar grid of numbered and lettered streets along with ample public squares, most of which endure today as city parks. In addition, the plan shows the S-curved old channel of the Sacramento River before its redirection, and the early extent of Sutter Lake, a slough that connected to the river. Also noteworthy is the absence of any bridges. Along the American River lies Sacramento's lone river crossing at the time—a ferry connecting to a road leading to "Feather River and the Mines." This ferry would be replaced in 1851 by Lisle's Bridge. Located on Sixteenth Street, the timber drawbridge was the first of its kind in the Sacramento River Delta. (LOC.)

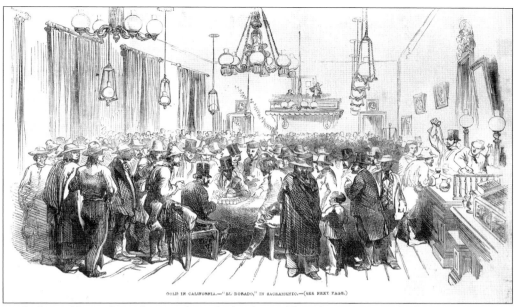

GOLD IN CALIFORNIA.—"EL DORADO," IN SACRAMENTO.—(SEE NEXT PAGE.)

With the sudden influx of miners brought by the Gold Rush, Sacramento ballooned in size and began to offer entertainment for its diverse, risk-taking new residents. Gambling halls and saloons, like the Round Tent and Jack's Saloon, lined Front Street, where men tried their hands at faro and monte. Depicted here is El Dorado Gambling Saloon at Second and J Streets. (LOC.)

PLACER TIMES.

VOL. I.   SACRAMENTO CITY, AUGUST 11, 1849.   NO. 14.

PLACER TIMES.

A WEEKLY NEWSPAPER,

Is printed and published at Sacramento City, Upper California, on Saturday of each week, by
T. R. PER LEE & Co.

Terms.

Subscription for one year, *in advance*, - - $10.00
"   " six months, - - 6.00
"   " three months, - - 4.00
Single copies, - - - - - - - - 25

Terms of Advertising.

For one square of 12 lines, (or less,) first insertion, $3.00
For every subsequent insertion, (per square,) 1.50
☞ All descriptions of Book and Job printing executed at the Placer Times office neatly, promptly and at reasonable rates.

Business Cards.

S. BRANNAN & Co.
Wholesale & Retail, Forwarding, Storage & Commission merchants.
Corner of Front and J sts., and at the
SUTTER'S FORT
sacramento city,   Apr. 28th

HENSLEY, READING, & Co
Wholesale & Retail Dealers,
sacramento city.   1-tf

MARSHALL & SANRTY,
*Wholesale and Retail Dealers in Dry Goods,
Groceries, &c.*
sacramento city.   2tf

VON PFISTER & VAUGHAN
*Dealers in dry goods, groceries and liquors.,
boots, shoes, and clothing, etc.*
Cash paid for gold dust.
EDWARD H VON PFISTER

Gold! Gold! Gold!—Everybody is leaving, or preparing to leave, for California, this new found El Dorado. Old men and young men, wise men and fools, rich and poor, are turning their eyes with longing toward this land of golden hopes. No less than twenty vessels of various sizes, are advertised to sail some time during next month, carrying out their freights of expectant gold seekers.

We have no doubt that the accounts regarding the abundance of gold in California, are mainly true; nor do we doubt that large quantities of the precious metal have been gathered by individuals without much labor. Still, we would advise those who are going out to the gold region to moderate their expectations. They should consider well their privations. They should bear in mind that in California there is yet no law but the will of the strongest, and that life and property are insecure, and that in the most favorable circumstances, they must labor harder, and fare worse than our Southern slaves, or state prison convicts. Then again, the climate is unhealthy and the cholera will find there an admirable sphere for its ravages during the ensuing summer. We dislike to be a prophet of evil, but we cannot forbear expressing the opinion that of those who go out to California, but few will return, and that those few will not be much richer than before.

We find the above in the Golden Rule, published in New York. The editor will not have much to "answer for" in the matter of inducing people to emigrate to this "glorious cou ry."

St. Louis. May 25.—Persons have arrived from the Plains, who state that the cholera had broken out among the mounted rifleman and emigrants. A company of New Yorkers numbering about thirty, had left twenty-five behind them. Their teams had given out, and their wagons were broken.

Twelve hundred emigrants were landed at St. Louis on the 10th and 11th May. They were just from Europe and shipboard, and brought sickness, disease and death with them. They quit of course the vessels as speedily as possible, and, go where they may, carry the seeds of disease with them.

There had been a heavy gale at Baltimore and many vessels were compelled to put back. It was feared that a number of vessels went ashore on the night of May 24.

The inhabitants of the south of France, Savoy, and a part of Italy, live almost exclusively on chestnuts during fall and early part of winter, making them into bread and puddings in place of flour. Nuts abound in vegetable oil, and of course in carbon, and also in glutine and fibrine, three of the most important elements required for sustaining life. Yet they should be dried or cooked.

The stock market in New York was very much depressed on the 25th of May, and the papers advise the board of brokers to adjourn till fall.

A duel was fought at San Francisco on Friday of last week. Both parties escaped without serious injury. The affair originated at a faro table.

The *Placer Times*, Sacramento's earliest newspaper, published its first issue on April 11, 1849. The 13-by-18-inch weekly, which was published every Saturday, was first printed in a one-story cabin at Sutter's Fort using a press once owned by California's first printer, Agustín V. Zamorano. Appropriate to the concerns of the time, this issue's lead article is headlined "Gold! Gold! Gold!"

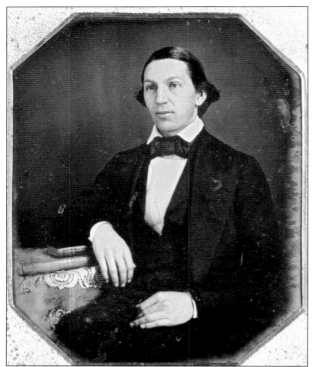

Rev. Joseph Augustine Benton arrived in Sacramento in July 1849, having served as minister to gold rushers aboard the *Edward Everett*. Shortly after his arrival, he established the first church in Sacramento, the First Church of Christ (Congregational). The church held its first meeting on September 16, 1849, in the city's first schoolhouse, which was located at the northeast corner of Third and I Streets. (CSL.)

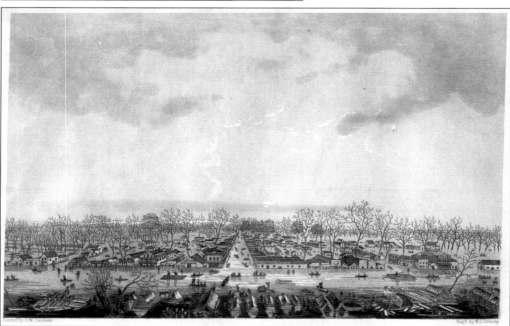

Floods, which would be a perennial problem for Sacramento, first tested the new city in January 1850. The Sacramento River rose above 30 feet, and floodwaters rushed in through the slough at I Street and over the levee. Many businesses near the river were submerged or carried off by the current, and houses, tents, trees, and livestock floated for miles inland.

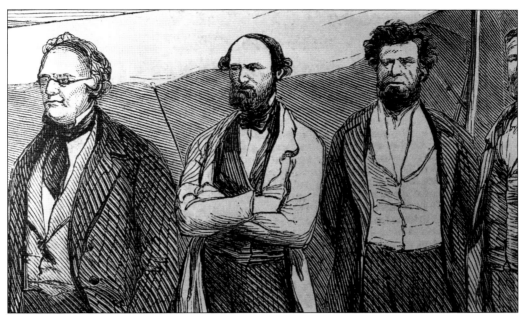

In August 1850, a group of settlers who claimed squatters' rights to John Sutter's former land grant confronted property speculators and city leaders in a deadly riot. The squatters rallied around Dr. Charles Robinson (center), who was later indicted and subsequently acquitted for murder, assault with the intent to kill, and conspiracy. While in jail onboard the *La Grange* prison ship awaiting trial, Robinson was elected to the state legislature.

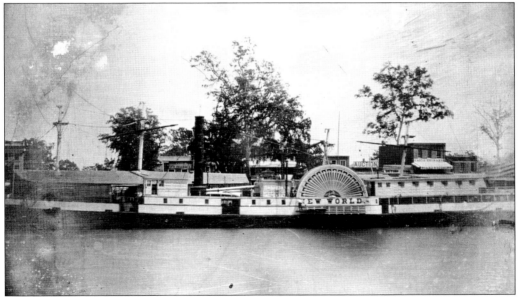

The earliest extant photograph of Sacramento, dating from around 1850, shows the *New World* steamer at the Sacramento levee. Shortly after this image was captured, a devastating cholera epidemic first appeared at the levee, initially spread by the schooner *G.H. Montague*. Several of the ship's passengers succumbed to the disease en route to San Francisco after departing Sacramento bound for New York on October 18, 1850. (CSH.)

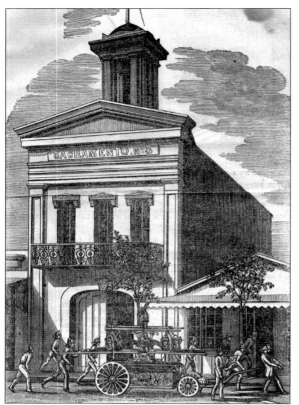

On April 4, 1850, Sacramento suffered losses from its first major fire. Citizens soon united to establish a fire organization, Sacramento Engine Co. No. 3. Located on Second Street, the company was one of three volunteer engine companies to form the core of Sacramento's first permanent fire department in March 1851. The Citizens' Fire Committee provided funds for the pictured engine house and ornately painted engine.

After recovering from a series of floods in 1850 and 1851, Sacramento awoke on the morning of November 3, 1852, to find a city laid in ruins by fire. Strong winds from the northwest aided the blaze, which ravaged the wood-built city within minutes of its spark at 11:00 p.m. the night before. The fire destroyed every public building save the Presbyterian church and courthouse.

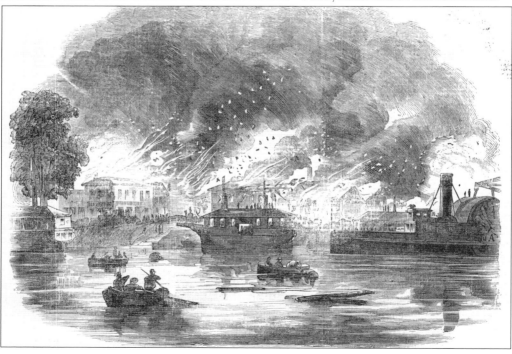

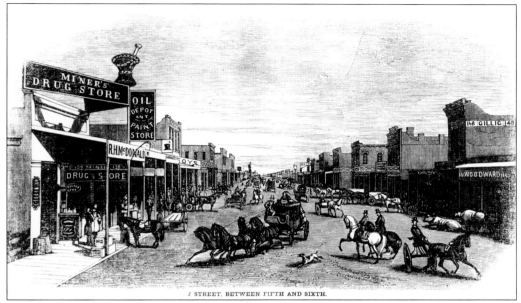

J STREET, BETWEEN FIFTH AND SIXTH.

Sacramento's business district was bustling in the early 1850s, as seen in this 1854 lithograph of J Street between Fifth and Sixth Streets. Businesses catering to miners, like the Miner's Drugstore, found great success in the post–Gold Rush period. Even the Big Four tycoons of the Central Pacific Railroad, Charles Crocker, Mark Hopkins, Collis Potter Huntington, and Leland Stanford, started their fortunes selling to miners at the Huntington, Hopkins & Co. and Stanford Brothers Store.

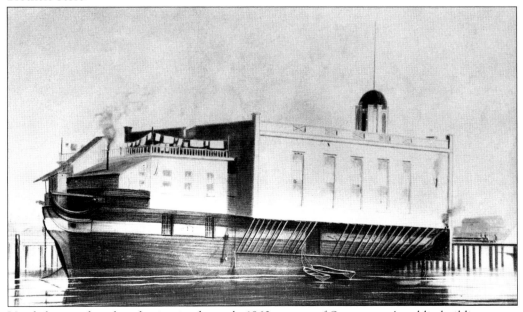

Until the city found its footing in the early 1860s, many of Sacramento's public buildings were temporary in nature. Prior to the construction of a proper jail, those awaiting trial were imprisoned aboard ship. The *La Grange* prison brig, pictured here, housed Sacramento County prisoners at the foot of H Street from 1850 until 1861–1862, when the vessel was sunk by the great flood. (CSL.)

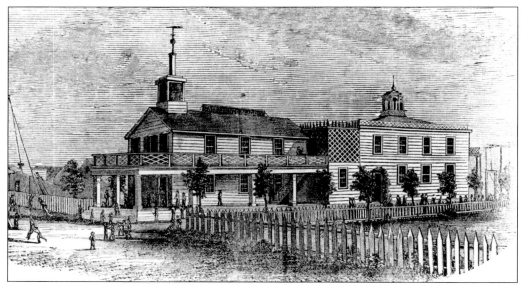

Sacramento High School opened September 1, 1856, on the campus of the Sacramento Academy and Female Institute. It is pictured here on M Street between Eighth and Ninth Streets. Of the 40 who initially applied for admission, 21 were admitted upon passing the entry examination in reading, orthography (spelling), arithmetic, geography, and grammar. (CSH.)

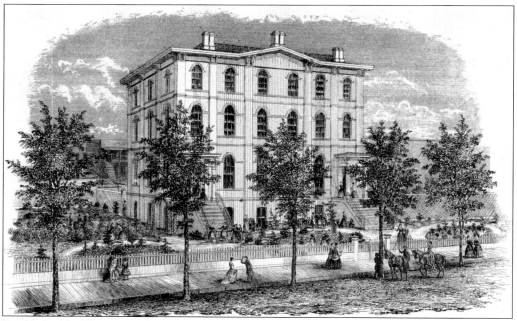

Established by Hermon and Nerina Perry in 1863, Sacramento Female Seminary was one of the largest schools in Sacramento to offer instruction at the secondary level. In 1868, the boarding and day school opened at this site on I Street between Tenth and Eleventh Streets. After the seminary closed, the building served as an educational center, later housing the city's night school and a Chinese public school.

United States Military Telegraph.

Received 3.30bm Oct 15. 1861.

From Sacremento 7.40 Pm Oct 24th

To Abraham Lincoln

In the temporary absence of the Governor of the State I am requested to send you the first message which will be transmitted over the wires of the telegraph line which Connect the Pacific with the Atlantic States, the People of California desire to Congratulate you upon the Completion of the great work.

They believe that it will be the means of stengthening the attachment which bind both the

12660

Before the transcontinental railroad made Sacramento a rail destination, the city was a hub of communication. The Wells Fargo Express office on J Street between Second and Third Streets served as the terminus of the Pony Express route from April to October 1861, while the Pioneer Telegraph Office on Second Street received the first message sent via transcontinental wire. On October 25, 1861, the telegraph connection linking Washington, DC, and Sacramento was completed, enabling California Chief Justice Stephen Field to send this message of support for the Union to Pres. Abraham Lincoln. Sacramento now had an instant connection to the Atlantic coast states, a significant improvement over the 10 days it took Pony Express riders to cross the continent. In the early days, the Sacramento telegraph office provided the rest of California with daily updates on the Civil War raging in the East. (LOC.)

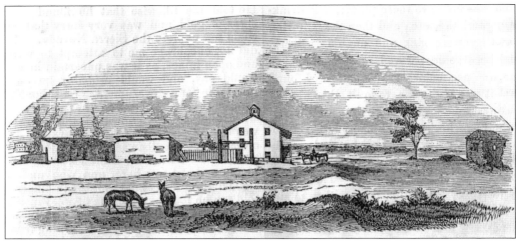

After 1850, when John Sutter sold most of his land holdings in the Sacramento area and retired to Hock Farm on the Feather River, Sutter's Fort quickly fell into disrepair. By 1857, when this sketch was completed, the fort's outer wall had fallen and only a few buildings remained standing.

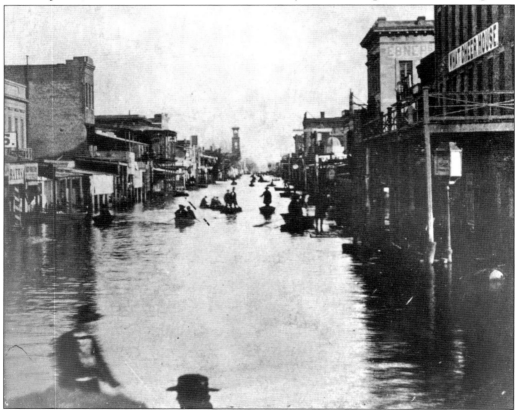

Until Sacramento's streets were raised in the late 1860s and early 1870s, seasonal flooding was a part of life for the river city. From December 1861 to January 1862, the largest flood in the recorded history of California swept through Sacramento. This view of flooding at Front and K Streets shows boat traffic through the business district.

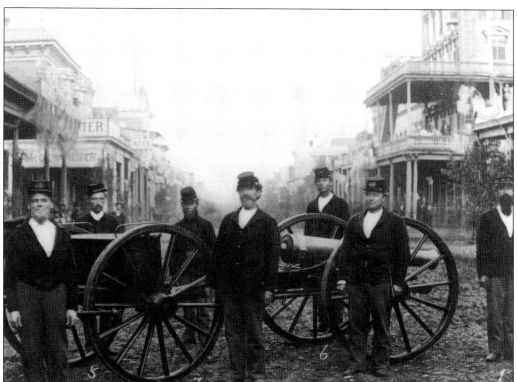

Uniformed militiamen pose here on K Street with "Union Boy," a 12-pound field gun that debuted on January 21, 1864. The purpose of the gun, which was purchased by W.M. Siddens, was to conduct salutes and proclaim Union victories in the city. During the Civil War, Sacramento claimed several pro-Union militia units and was also home to Camp Union, a training center located at Sutterville. (CSH.)

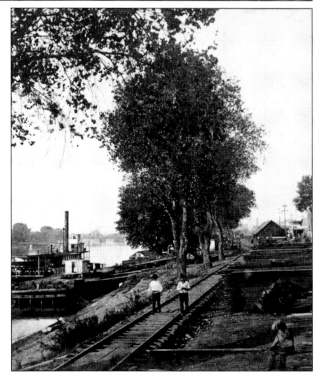

A riverboat and a lumberyard frame rail tracks south of Front Street in this c. 1864 image. Sacramento developed a robust industrial strip along the Sacramento River in the 1850s and early 1860s. Along with lumberyards, numerous factories and foundries sprung up south of L Street, while several of the biggest gristmills in the state were situated on the waterfront to the north. (CSL.)

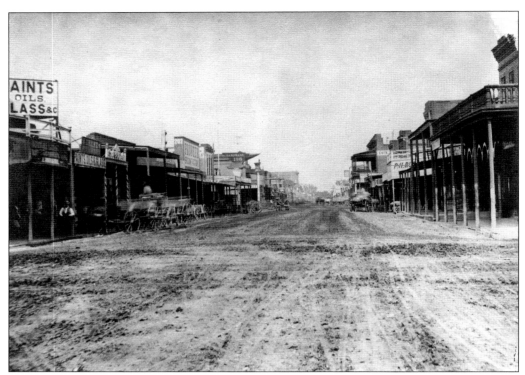

Covered plank sidewalks fronted brick buildings bearing signs of all shapes and sizes on J Street in the 1860s. This photograph, taken from Eighth Street looking west, shows humble businesses selling an assortment of goods, from brooms to paints to hardware. This block marked the eastern bounds of Sacramento's business district. (CSL.)

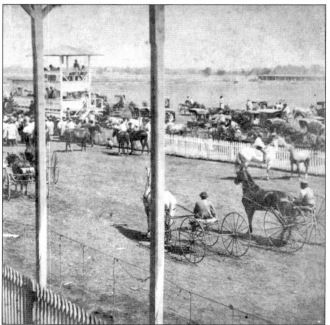

Boulevard Park was on the outskirts of the city in the 1850s and 1860s and was home to Sacramento's Union Park Racecourse, pictured here in 1870. Located in Agricultural Park, the track hosted California State Fair horse races until 1904. Famed photographer Edward Muybridge's first attempt at capturing horses galloping in motion took place at the course just two years after this photograph was taken.

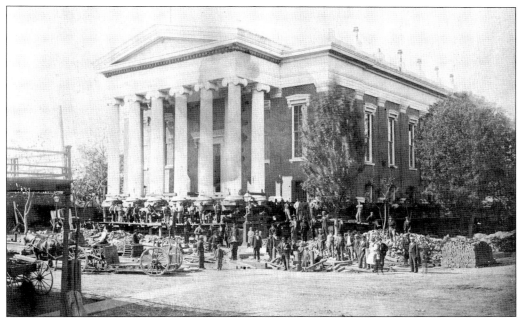

The Sacramento County Courthouse, which was constructed at the corner of Seventh and I Streets in 1854, was raised and remodeled in 1870 to meet the new street grade. Sacramento had commenced raising the city streets several blocks inland from the Sacramento River in 1863 in order to avoid catastrophic flooding. (CSL.)

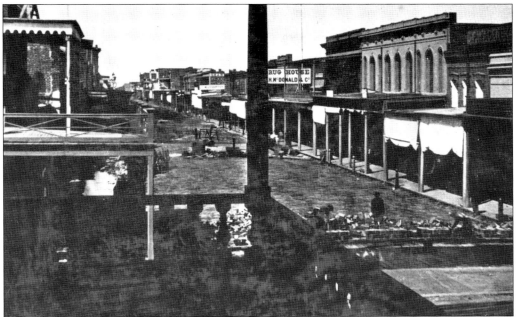

After raising city streets in the 1860s, the City of Sacramento contracted out to pave them. Pictured here are crews laying Nicolson pavement along J Street near Sixth Street. Nicolson pavement and Stowe pavement (invented by Sacramentan H.M. Stowe) consisted of wooden blocks and covered many blocks of J and K Streets until the late 1870s, when they were replaced with cobbles.

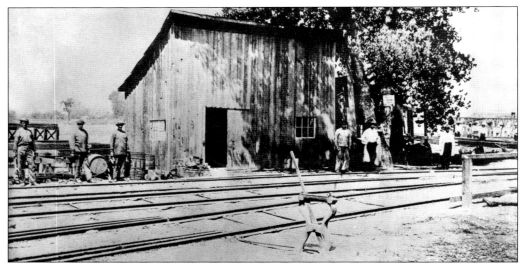

Central Pacific Railroad (CP) laid the first rail of the transcontinental railroad in California in late October 1863. Over the following six years, CP constructed the rail line, bridges, depots, and shops in Sacramento. The railroad's first depot and ticket office in Sacramento, pictured here at Front and I Streets in 1863, was built in one afternoon at a cost of $150.

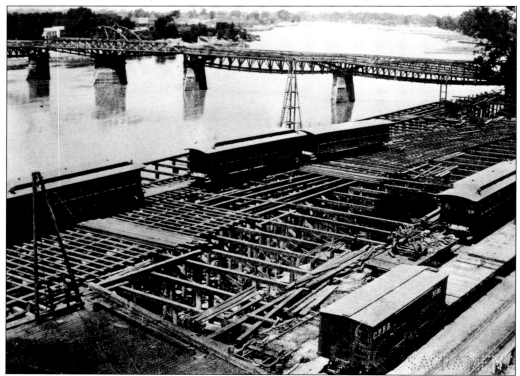

Construction of the Sacramento River waterfront near I Street is shown in this c. 1864 image. The old grade of the levee, sloping toward the Sacramento River, is just visible below the boardwalk. Sacramento's first bridge across the Sacramento River, which opened in 1858, also can be seen extending across the river to Yolo County.

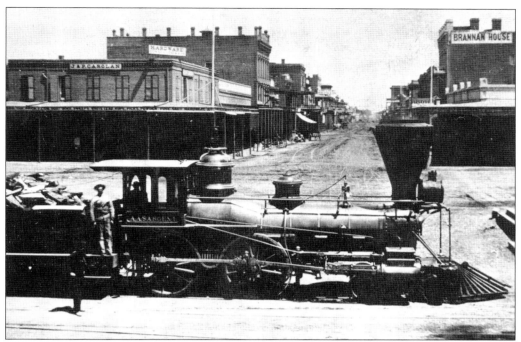

Central Pacific Railroad's first California-built locomotive, the *A.A. Sargent*, runs along Front Street at the foot of J Street in this 1865 image. The engine was initially built for the Sacramento Valley Railroad, California's first short line railway, which ran from Folsom to Sacramento. The locomotive was named after the US representative from California who authored the Pacific Railroad Act, which promoted construction of a transcontinental railroad.

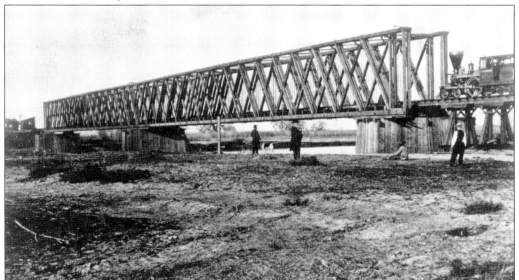

The first railroad bridge across the American River in Sacramento was constructed in 1864. The wooden truss bridge, built by Hubbard and Baker near the site of present-day Cal Expo, was about 400 feet long. Pictured at right is the *C.P. Huntington* locomotive preparing to cross the new bridge around the time of its opening.

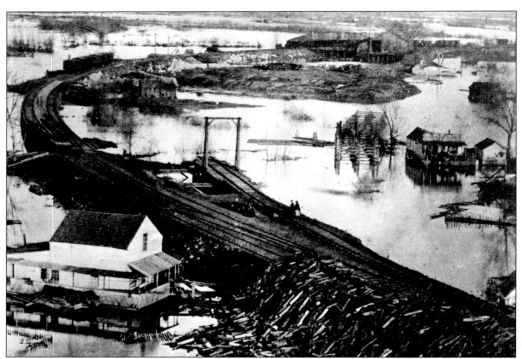

Sutter Lake, popularly called China Slough beginning in the 1870s, was located at a site later occupied by the Southern Pacific Railroad shops (from the Sacramento River to Sixth Street and between F and I Streets). Initially, it connected to the Sacramento River and expanded with every flood—like the one pictured here in 1868.

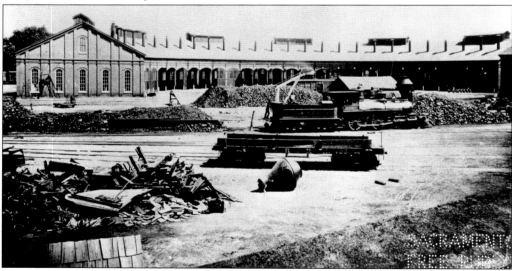

The roundhouse of the Central Pacific Railroad opened in 1868 and directed engines in for maintenance until its shuttering in the late 1950s. Twenty-nine tracks led outward from the 56-foot turntable into the roundhouse stalls. It was the largest roundhouse constructed for the transcontinental railroad and formed the nucleus of what would become the largest railroad facility in the West.

Since the city's formation, J and K Streets were lined with Sacramento's most prominent businesses and institutions. Alongside many businesses stands St. Rose of Lima, which was founded in 1854 as Sacramento's first Catholic church. The church is seen in this early image of K Street. Across the street is the Golden Eagle Hotel at 617 K Street, which had housed Sacramento notables since 1850.

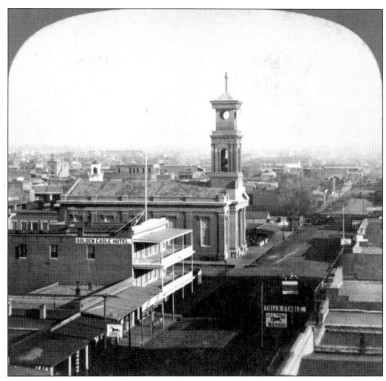

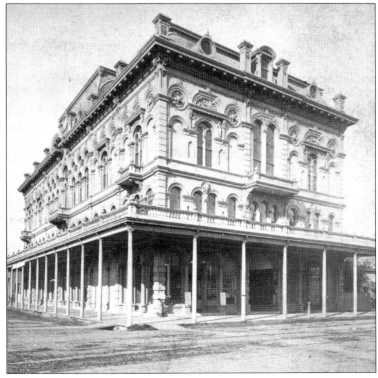

In 1869, the Odd Fellows contracted local architect Adam Kinkle to design this new hall at the northeast corner of Ninth and K Streets. At the time of its opening, it was one of the grandest buildings in the city. The Odd Fellows formed the first benevolent association in Sacramento in 1850 to raise money to build a hospital for those suffering from the cholera epidemic. (CSL.)

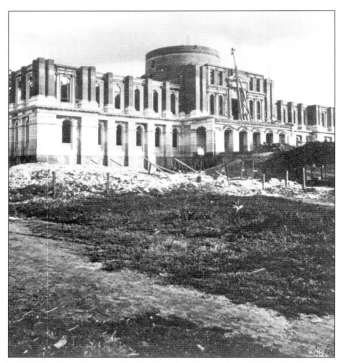

Although San Jose, Benicia, and Vallejo each hosted legislative sessions after California became a state in 1850, the capitol settled in Sacramento for good in 1854, first making its home in the Sacramento County Courthouse on I Street. Construction began on the present neoclassical capitol in 1861, though it paused as resources became scarce during the Civil War. The capitol is pictured at left under construction in the early 1860s and below near completion in 1869, as viewed looking southeast from Tenth and L Streets. Construction was completed in 1874, and the Constitutional Convention of 1879 declared Sacramento the permanent state capitol.

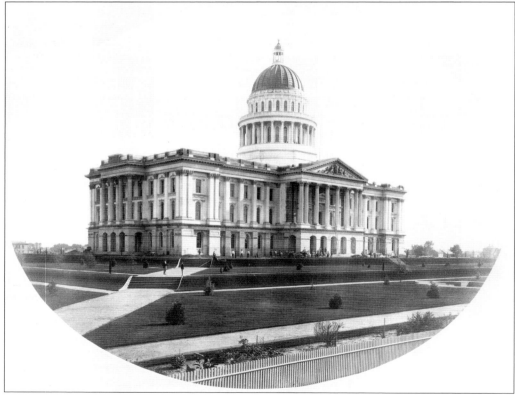

Two

THE AGE OF ACHIEVEMENT
1870 TO 1915

Sacramento experienced a period of rapid development during the late 1800s and early 1900s, stimulated by several major technological advances. By 1869, the city had become the western terminus of the first transcontinental railroad, and the need had developed for a workforce capable of building and repairing locomotives. About 3,000 men were employed in the Southern Pacific Railroad shops by 1883, making the railroad one of Sacramento's largest employers. Immigrant groups such as the Irish, many having arrived during the Gold Rush, filled these railroad jobs in the early years. Other industries, including flour mills, expanded to support the growing population. By 1878, there were eight breweries in the area.

New developments in shipping, such as the refrigerated railroad car, kindled the growth of agriculture as another mainstay of the local economy. The connections created by the railroad, as well as by steamships navigating the Sacramento River, made it possible to export agricultural products throughout the country and abroad. New technology brought more changes with the introduction of electricity in 1895, achieved by the first transmission of hydroelectric power, some 22 miles from the Folsom Powerhouse to Sacramento. In 1870, residents experienced a new mobility when public streetcars were introduced using horse-drawn trolleys, which would adapt to electric power in the 1890s. Automobiles made their debut when the first dealership opened in 1903, with 27 vehicles registered in the county by 1905.

As the city grew, many of its institutions were created. Iconic buildings that were completed during this period include the California State Capitol in 1874, the Cathedral of the Blessed Sacrament in 1889, and city hall in 1911. In 1879, voters approved the opening of the Free Public Library, which would be located at Eighth and I Streets. The California State Fair moved to its new home in the magnificent Agricultural Pavilion in Capitol Park in 1884. The Crocker Art Gallery was gifted to the city by Margaret Crocker in 1885 to become a museum. The Native Sons of the Golden West purchased the remains of Sutter's Fort, donating it to the State of California in 1891 with an eye to ensuring its preservation. Although challenges still existed, Sacramento was clearly thriving.

—Elizabeth Daugherty

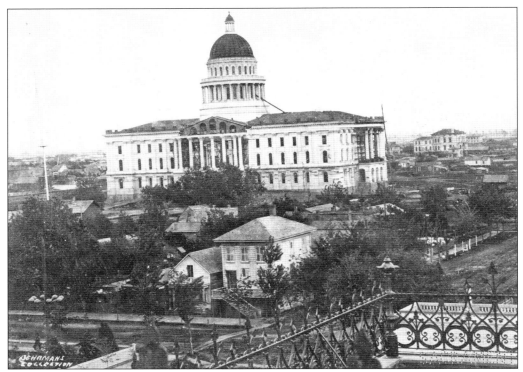

Although the state legislature approved the construction of the California State Capitol by 1860, there were delays in the project, such as the one caused by serious flooding in 1861–1862. Taken from the Leland Stanford home at Eighth and N Streets, this c. 1873 photograph shows continuing construction on the capitol, which was completed in 1874. The state printing plant is seen in the background on the right.

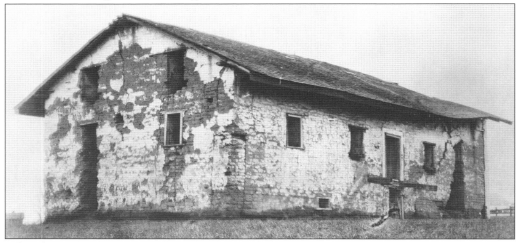

After the formation of Sacramento proper, Sutter's Fort was abandoned and fell into disrepair. Left to the elements and scavengers, its central building, shown in 1879, was all that remained. By 1890, interest in restoring the fort had grown and the Native Sons of the Golden West raised $20,000 to purchase the property. The fort was donated to the state in 1891, and reconstruction began in the 1890s. (CSL.)

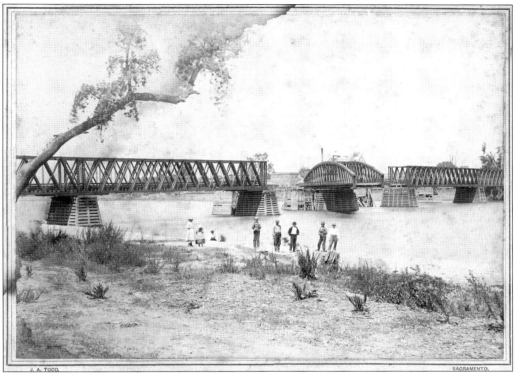

This 1870s photograph shows the city's first railroad bridge to be built across the Sacramento River. Constructed in 1870 by the Central Pacific Railroad, it was the second bridge at this location, which would eventually be the site of the I Street Bridge. This wooden truss bridge had a single railroad track that accommodated mixed traffic. The children in this photograph are on the west bank of the river. (CSL.)

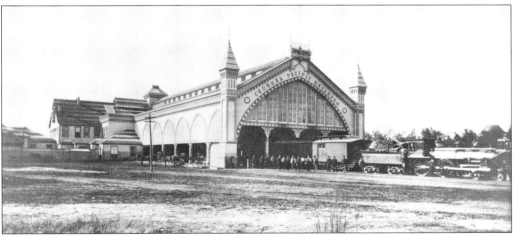

Known as the "Arcade Station," the Gothic-style Central Pacific Railroad depot, seen here in 1882, was located on G Street between Second and Third Streets. Constructed in 1879, this modern station had three tracks, a 150-seat dining room, and distinctive twin spires. The Arcade Station was the city's third Central Pacific/Southern Pacific depot and was replaced by the new railroad station at Fourth and I Streets in 1925.

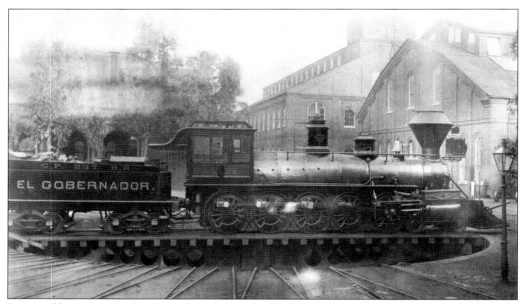

Designed by master mechanic Andrew J. Stevens and built in Sacramento in 1883, Central Pacific steam locomotive No. 237, *El Gobernador*, was the largest of its time and was the last locomotive to receive an official name. This 1885 view of the locomotive shows the Sacramento railroad shops in the background, including the roundhouse, car shop, and machine shop. *El Gobernador* was dismantled on July 15, 1894.

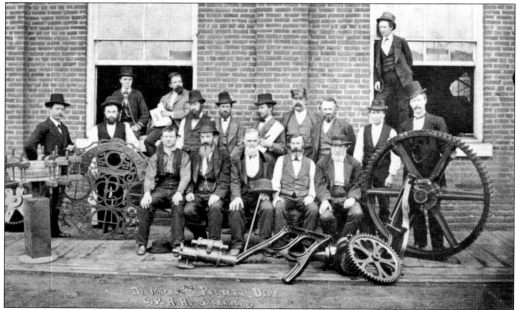

Displaying several items representing their craft, these men were employed at the Central Pacific railyards in the designers and pattern department in 1876. A pattern-maker, working at one of many trades needed to operate the shops, used drawings to create wooden patterns that would be used to cast parts for locomotives. Among those posing for this photograph were George Stoddard, C.T. Noyes, Max Eichrodt, and Ed Schnauss. (CSH.)

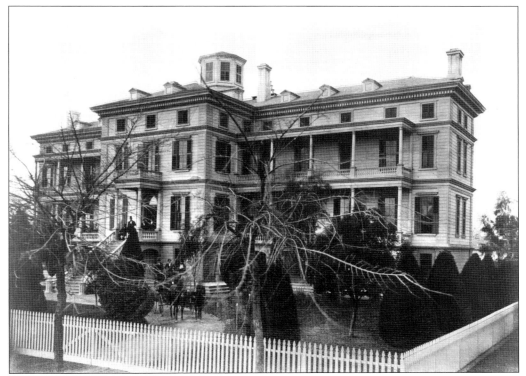

One of Sacramento's early hospitals was built to address the health care needs of injured and ill railroad workers, who often otherwise lacked this support. The 125-bed Central Pacific Railroad Hospital, seen in this c. 1875 photograph, opened in 1869 at the corner of Thirteenth and C Streets. The employer collected dues of 50¢ a month from its workers to provide medical services at the hospital and in residences. (CSH.)

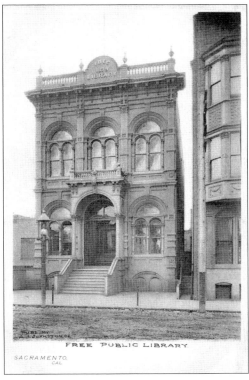

FREE PUBLIC LIBRARY.

SACRAMENTO, CAL.

No longer satisfied with the members-only, fee-based library opened in 1857, Sacramento's citizens voted in 1879 for a free public library that would serve all residents. The Sacramento Library Association transferred its building and collection to the City of Sacramento, and the Sacramento Free Public Library opened June 14, 1879, with a collection of approximately 6,000 volumes. This c. 1915 postcard shows the library at 718 I Street.

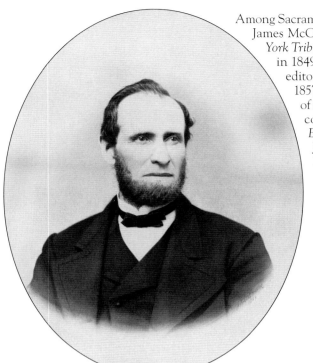

Among Sacramento's early benefactors was Irish-born James McClatchy (1824–1883). The former *New York Tribune* editor, who arrived in Sacramento in 1849 to mine for gold, became the second editor of the *Sacramento Bee* newspaper in 1857. As McClatchy promoted the interests of Sacramento's citizens against powerful corporations and the government, the *Bee* found its progressive voice. After James's death in 1883, sons Charles Kenny and Valentine assumed the *Sacramento Bee*'s leadership. (CSL.)

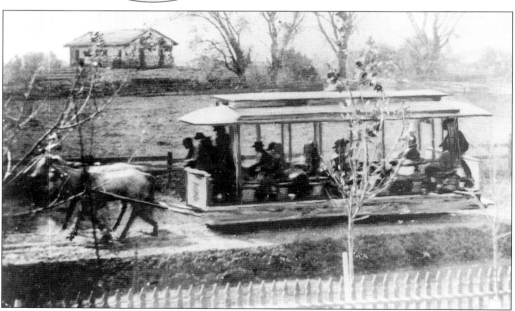

Before steam-generated electricity became its power source in 1890, Sacramento's streetcar system consisted of horse-drawn carriages. The omnibus in this c. 1888 photograph is traveling east on J Street between Twenty-Seventh and Twenty-Eighth Streets. In the background are the remains of the central building of Sutter's Fort, which later underwent a restoration set in motion by the Sacramento Pioneers and the Native Sons of the Golden West.

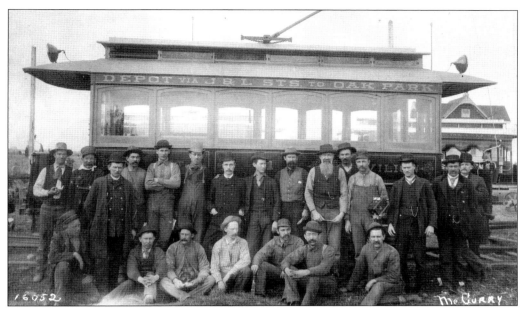

With tools in hand, Central Street Railway workers pose in front of Car No. 1 on the M Street line, seen at the Oak Park Pavilion in the 1890s. This line ran from the Central Pacific Railroad depot downtown to the Oak Park terminus. Later purchased by the Sacramento Electric, Gas & Railway Company, the Central Street Railway Company pioneered the use of electricity to power streetcars in Sacramento. (CSL.)

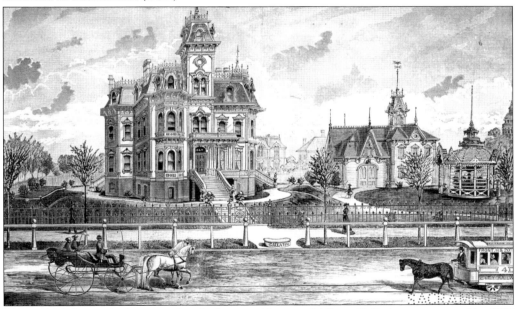

This 1880 lithograph shows, in detail, the grand home of Albert Gallatin, constructed in 1877 at 1527 H Street. Gallatin, president of Sacramento Power and Light Company, pioneered the development of hydroelectric power. Purchased in 1903 by the State of California, the mansion served as the residence of 13 California governors between 1903 and 1967. In 2015, Gov. Jerry Brown and Anne Gust Brown made the renovated mansion their home.

41

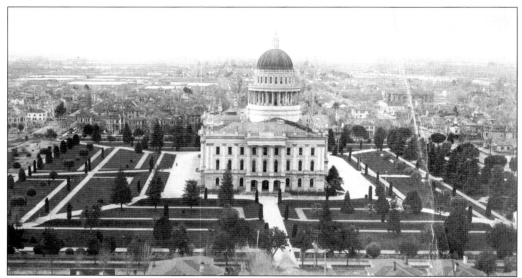

For many years, Sacramento's residents and visitors alike have enjoyed Capitol Park, prominent in this c. 1880 view looking south from Eleventh Street. Laid out in a formal geometric pattern, the park's original boundaries of N, L, Tenth, and Twelfth Streets expanded to Fifteenth Street in the 1880s when it served as the site of the California State Fair. The park now features several monuments and trees from around the world.

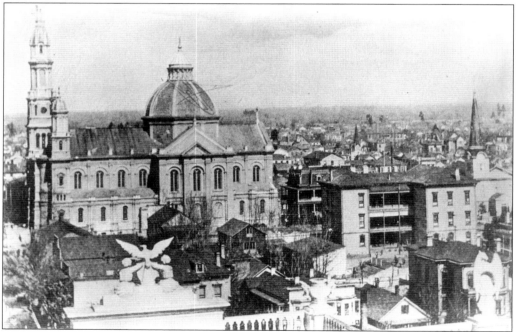

Constructed between 1886 and 1889 at Eleventh and K Streets, the Cathedral of the Blessed Sacrament was designed to resemble the Church of the Holy Trinity in Paris. This January 1900 photograph was taken from the California State Capitol looking north. To the right of the cathedral is the German Evangelical Church at Twelfth and K Streets. The cathedral is the seat of the Catholic Diocese of Sacramento.

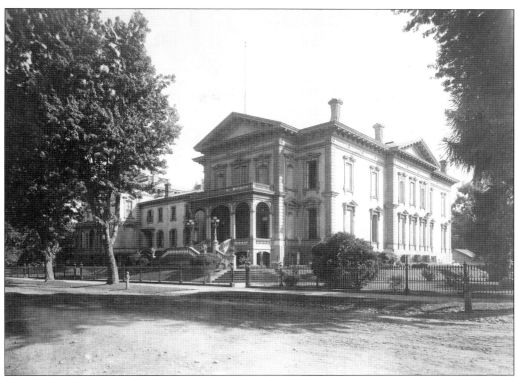

With his wife, Margaret, Judge Edwin Bryant Crocker of the Central Pacific Railroad used his fortune to build a remarkable art collection during the 1860s. The couple traveled throughout Europe acquiring paintings and hired architect Seth Babson to design this elegant gallery at 216 O Street to showcase their collection. Seen around 1915, it is now the Crocker Art Museum, one of the longest continuously operating art museums in the West. (CSL.)

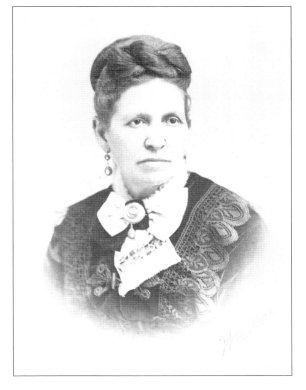

Seen in this 1870 portrait, Margaret Crocker became a major Sacramento philanthropist after the 1875 death of her husband, Edwin Bryant Crocker. After she gifted her family's collection of art to the city to start a museum, Sacramentans thanked her by holding the Festival of Flowers on May 6, 1885. She also donated land to the city cemetery, and in 1884 opened the Marguerite Home for older, impoverished women. (CSL.)

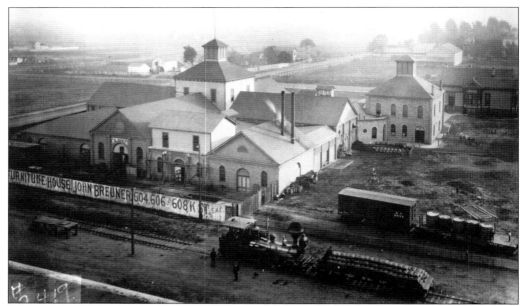

Several commercial wineries flourished in the Sacramento area during the late 1800s. Built in 1871 on Twenty-First Street between R and S Streets, the Eberhardt and Lachman Winery was renamed the California Winery when Portuguese immigrant Manuel Nevis purchased it in 1888. Experiencing changes in name and ownership, the winery produced 1.5 million gallons of wine in 1905 under the Cordova label. Prohibition led to its closure in 1926. (CSL.)

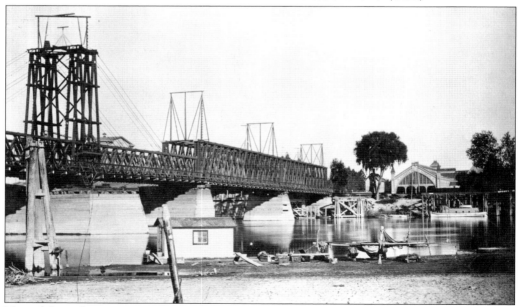

Viewed from the Sacramento River's west bank, this wooden railroad bridge was constructed in 1878, replacing the 1870 Central Pacific Railroad span. The new bridge accommodated trains and wagons on a single deck. In 1895, the bridge was replaced again, with a wooden two-deck structure that had two railroad tracks on its lower deck and a wagon road above. The railroad's Arcade Station is seen on the right, around 1885.

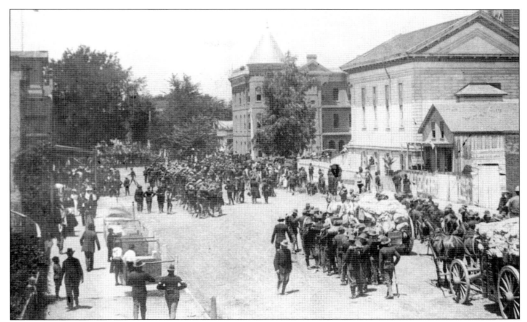

By 1894, the railroad employed approximately one third of Sacramento's workforce. An 1893 depression caused a drop in Pullman car sales, resulting in deep cuts in railroad employees' wages, while rents remained high in company-owned housing. Many of Sacramento's suffering railroad workers joined the strike called by the American Railway Union and socialist leader Eugene Debs. This photograph shows National Guard members at Sixth and L Streets during the Pullman Strike. (CSH.)

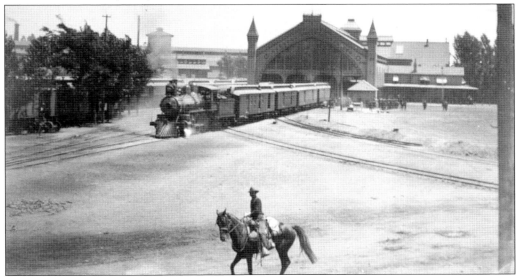

In June 1894, Sacramento railroad workers joined the nationwide Pullman Strike, refusing to move trains with Pullman cars. After days of escalating tension between strikers and federal troops, the situation reached its violent peak on July 11, 1894. That day, the train seen here was sabotaged three miles west of Sacramento, killing engineer Sam Clark and four US soldiers. Support for the strikers soon weakened, and rail service resumed. (CSH.)

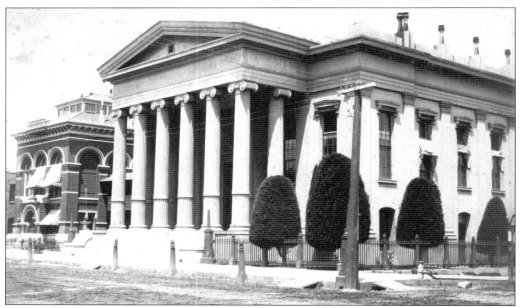

Constructed in 1855 at Seventh and I Streets, the second Sacramento County Courthouse was designed by architect David Farquharson. The building also functioned as the state capitol until 1869. On the left, connected to the courthouse by elevated walkway, is the hall of records. Completed in 1882, it was home to Sacramento County's offices. The third county courthouse was built at this location in 1913. (CSL.)

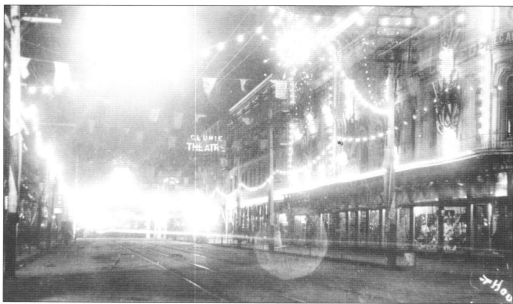

The Grand Electric Carnival was one of Sacramento's most spectacular celebrations. Held on September 9, 1895, in conjunction with the California State Fair and California Admission Day, the event celebrated the first transmission of hydroelectric power from the Folsom Powerhouse to Sacramento on July 15 of that year. On the right, on K Street between Eighth and Ninth Streets, are the Hale Bros. department store and the Clunie Theater.

This invitation to the September 9, 1895, Grand Electric Carnival used artwork to convey the magnitude of the July 15 transmission of hydroelectric power 22 miles from the Folsom Powerhouse to Sacramento. The accomplishment was celebrated as the first hydroelectric power transmission of this distance. The carnival featured a night parade of illuminated floats on light-draped streets. The imposing state capitol, outlined in lights, was visible from a distance of 50 miles.

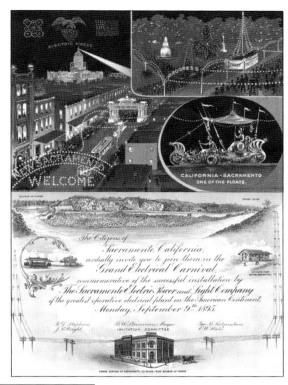

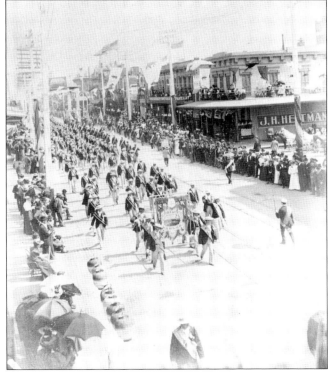

This September 9, 1895, photograph shows members of the Sacramento parlor, or chapter, of the Native Sons of the Golden West marching in the parade commemorating California's admission into the Union. The parade also celebrated the transmission of hydroelectric power 22 miles from the Folsom Powerhouse to Sacramento's Station "A" that year. Marching at Sixth and J Streets, members carry a banner that reads, "NSGW Sacramento Parlor."

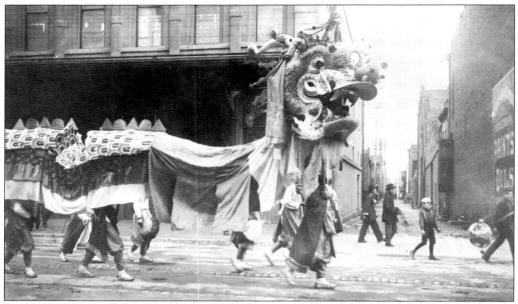

Sacramento's Chinese community celebrated the transmission of hydroelectric power from the Folsom Powerhouse to Sacramento by participating in the September 9, 1895, parade. This photograph shows marchers and a dragon at Second Street between I and J Streets. Many workers who constructed Folsom's dam, canal, and powerhouse came from Sacramento's Chinese community. Despite increased efforts to exclude them, Sacramento's Chinese residents continued to help build the city's foundation. (CSH.)

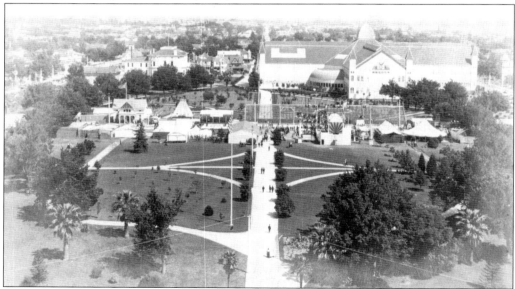

The California State Fair drew large crowds in its first long-term home in Capitol Park, seen looking east from the state capitol in 1890. The magnificent Agricultural Pavilion, built in 1884 at Fifteenth and N Streets, housed fair exhibits and hosted other events. In 1908, the pavilion was razed, the fair was relocated to Stockton Boulevard, and attendance increased. This photograph also shows the state printing office on the left.

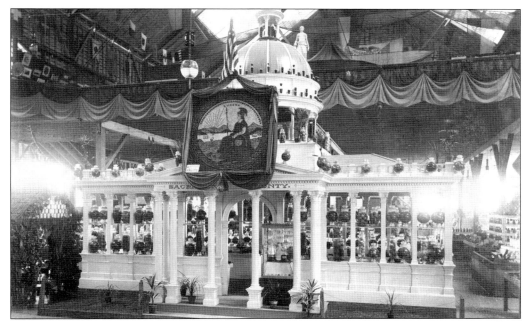

Having rotated to a different city each year since 1854, the California State Fair was held in Sacramento in 1859 at the city's first Agricultural Pavilion at Sixth and M Streets. Highlighting the area's agricultural products, this Sacramento County exhibit at the 1895 fair used an authentic scale model of the state capitol dome and a reproduction of the state seal to showcase a display of local fruit in glass canisters.

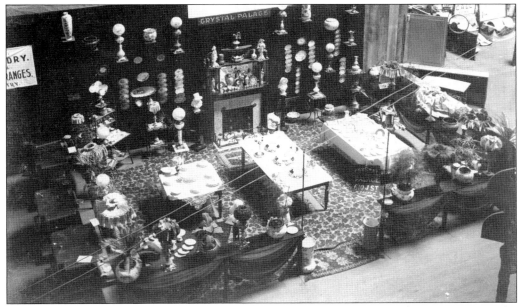

The Crystal Palace Pottery, located at 610 J Street in Sacramento, enjoyed great success at the 1895 California State Fair. The company's exhibit won awards for best display in the categories of ornamental statuary, Japanese ware, lamps, and others. After rotating to different cities, the fair made Sacramento its permanent home in 1861.

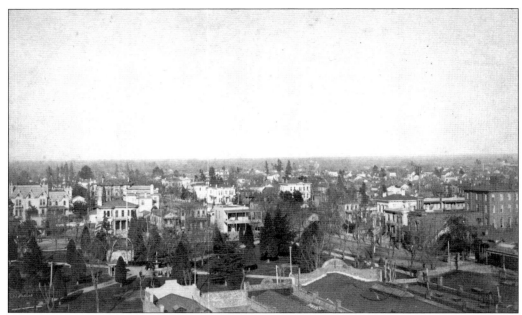

Long a site for community gatherings, Plaza Park is shown in this 1895 view. The park, situated in Sacramento's center between I, J, Ninth, and Tenth Streets, was one of 10 public squares set aside by John Sutter Jr. in 1849 for public use. A proposal to construct the state capitol here was abandoned in 1857. The park was renamed Cesar Chavez Plaza in 1999.

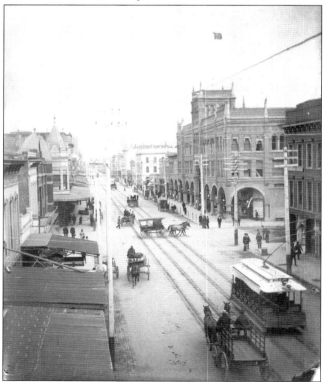

After a rare hailstorm, downtown visitors go their way at the intersection of K and Fourth Streets, the focus of this c. 1896 photograph. Horse-drawn wagons and an electric streetcar pass stores, including Weinstock, Lubin, and Co., seen on the right at the southeast corner of Fourth and K Streets. This three-story structure, the second Weinstock, Lubin, and Co. store, opened in 1891 and was destroyed by fire on January 31, 1903.

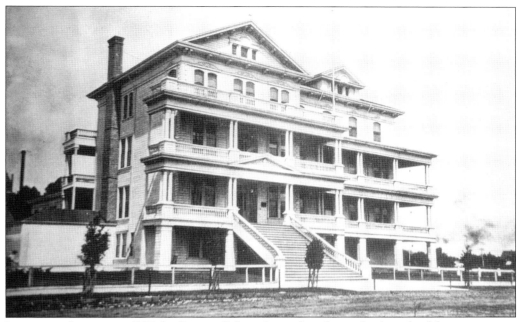

Longtime educators, in 1895 the Sisters of Mercy focused on the medical needs of the community. Purchasing the Ridge Home sanitarium at Twenty-Third and R Streets, they opened the 30-bed Mater Misericordiae Hospital on the site in 1897. As Sacramento's first private hospital, it was one of the most modern and well equipped in California. Seen in 1901, Mater Misericordiae (Latin for "Mother of Mercy") was known as "Sisters Hospital." (CSL.)

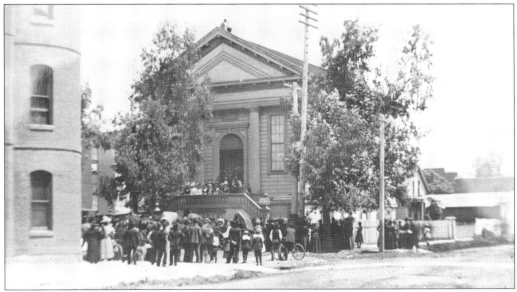

The first home of Westminster Presbyterian Church, seen around 1900, was a wooden structure built in 1867 at Sixth and L Streets. Located in what was considered a disreputable area, this building was replaced in 1904 by a more modern church at Thirteenth and K Streets. In 1927, the congregation found its current home in the beautiful Byzantine-style church designed by architect Charles F. Dean at Thirteenth and N Streets.

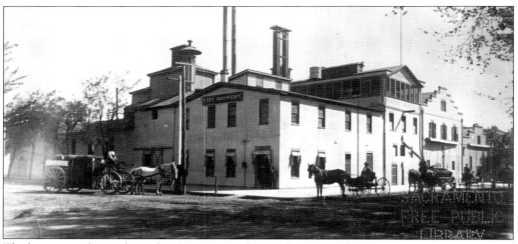

The brewing industry thrived in Sacramento during the city's early years. Pictured in this c. 1900 photograph is the City Brewery, built in 1856 at Twelfth and H Streets by German immigrants Wilhelm Borchers and Benedict Hilbert. In 1865, Swiss émigré Frank Ruhstaller became the foreman at the City Brewery, which he purchased in 1881. Ruhstaller later started his own brewing label and became majority shareholder in the Buffalo Brewery.

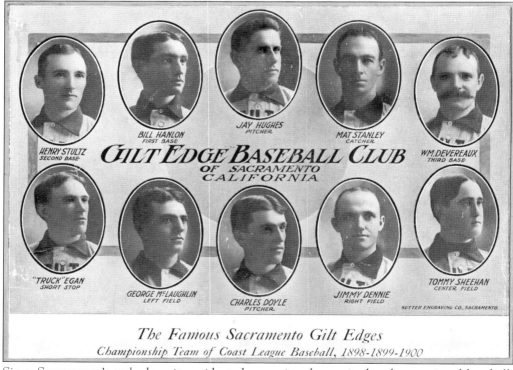

Since Sacramento's early days, its residents have enjoyed organized and recreational baseball. The Gilt Edge baseball club, formed in 1898 and sponsored by the local Ruhstaller Brewery, was named after the company's Gilt Edge Lager. This 1900 image shows the members of the team, which won league championships in 1898, 1899, and 1900. Despite its impressive record, the Gilt Edge team was reorganized and named the Senators in 1901.

Shiloh Baptist Church, founded in 1856 by Sacramento's African American community, was first located at Sixth and H Streets. When this photograph was taken around 1902, the church was located on the northwest corner of P and Sixth Streets. These church choir members are, from left to right, (first row), Lucy Ray, Reverend McPherson (minister of Shiloh Baptist Church), and Maude Ray; (second row), Delia Collins, unidentified, and May Russell. (CSH.)

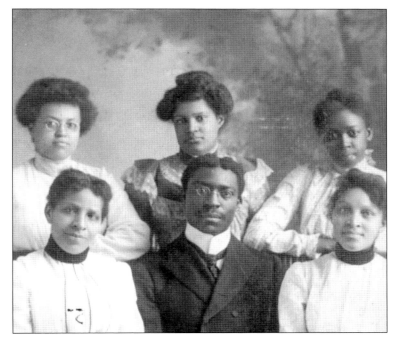

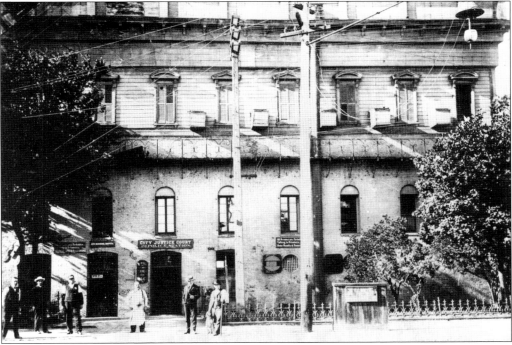

Sacramento's first municipal building, seen around 1900, was built in 1854 at Front and I Streets at a cost of $120,000. Serving many functions, it housed the mayor's office, police station, jail, justice court, fire department, receiving hospital, and the city's water supply, which was stored in rooftop tanks. Structural damage to the building led to the relocation of most city offices to 426 J Street by 1909. (CSH.)

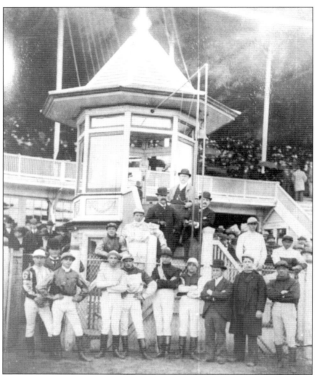

The California State Agricultural Society, which managed the annual California State Fair, opened Agricultural Park between B and H and Twentieth and Twenty-Third Streets in 1861. The park's many features included a racetrack and grandstand for spectators to watch horse and dog races. This c. 1900 photograph identifies jockeys and others at the racetrack, including J.W. Wilson, Dick Harvey, David Ahern, Tod Sloan, Alphonse Chevalier, and African American jockey Jerry Chon. (CSH.)

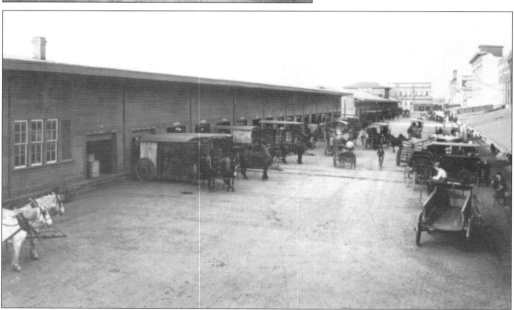

This active scene shows freight being transferred from warehouses to horse-drawn wagons along Front Street around 1900. The city's connections to San Francisco and other ports along the Sacramento River and its ability to ship goods long distances by rail helped it thrive commercially. In this photograph looking north, Sacramento's early city hall and waterworks building can be seen in the distance. (CSH.)

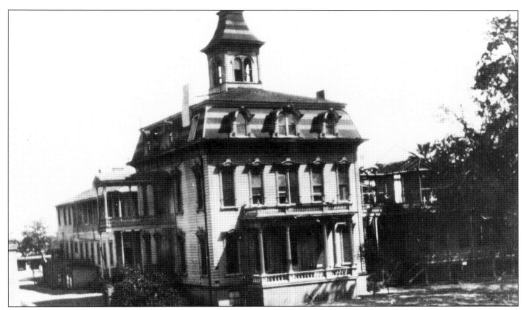

Sacramento County residents with limited support could receive medical care at the county hospital, situated outside the city limits on Stockton Boulevard. Replacing the original 1871 hospital destroyed by fire, this 1879 structure had five spoke-like wings, designed to increase access to sunlight. Seen here in 1900, the institution became a teaching hospital in the 1960s, partnering with the University of California, Davis. (BRUC.)

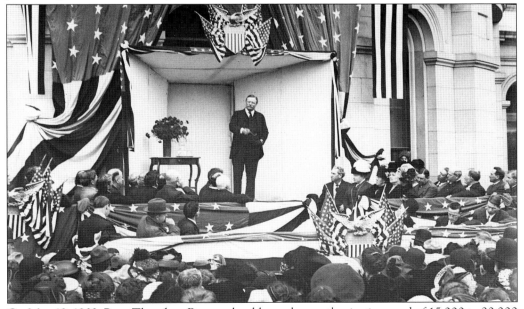

On May 19, 1903, Pres. Theodore Roosevelt addressed an enthusiastic crowd of 15,000 to 20,000 people on the steps of the California State Capitol. It was thought then to be the largest crowd ever gathered in Sacramento. Roosevelt was enjoying his first visit to California, stopping at Yosemite and several cities. On the day of his speech at the capitol, the Sacramento Pioneer Association awarded the president honorary membership. (CSL.)

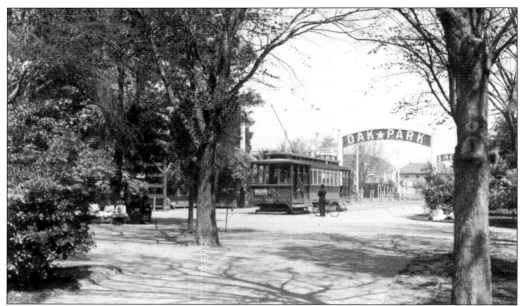

This peaceful c. 1903 view captures the beauty of Oak Park, with Car No. 14 of the Sacramento Electric, Gas & Railway Company in the background. This trolley followed the P Street route to the park and neighborhood, which were outside the city limits at the time. Oak Park was designed by developer Edwin Alsip in the 1880s and was annexed by the city in 1911, along with neighboring East Sacramento. (CSH.)

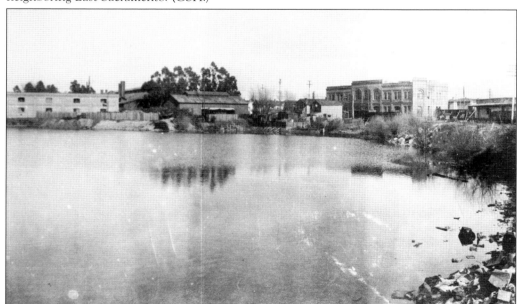

In 1904, the Southern Pacific Railroad signed a contract with Sacramento to drain China Lake (also known as Sutter Lake). The city deeded some of the land to the railroad for a future depot, which opened in 1925. After delays caused by equipment failure and other problems, the lake was filled by 1911. On the right in this 1905 photograph is Pacific Gas and Electric's two-story "gas house," later known as Station A. (CSH.)

Sacramento's German community came together to worship and socialize at the German Evangelical Church, seen here in 1907. Constructed in 1873 on the northeast corner of Twelfth and K Streets, the church and its congregation thrived under the leadership of the Rev. Charles Oehler, who arrived in 1890. In 1912, a majestic new Neo-Gothic structure was built at 1701 L Street. It was renamed St. John's Lutheran Church in 1919. (CSL.)

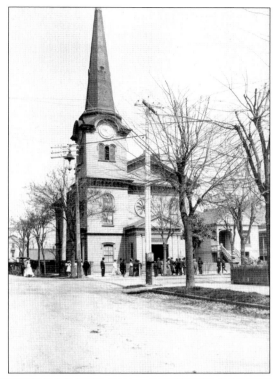

Arriving in 1857, the Catholic Sisters of Mercy assisted Sacramentans in need, mainly in the Alkali Flat neighborhood. After establishing their first school at St. Rose of Lima Church, they opened St. Joseph's Academy at Eighth and G Streets in 1861. This 1909 view shows the building, constructed in 1875, which accommodated 220 students, including 20 boarders. Replaced by a new structure in 1926, the school operated until 1966. (CSH.)

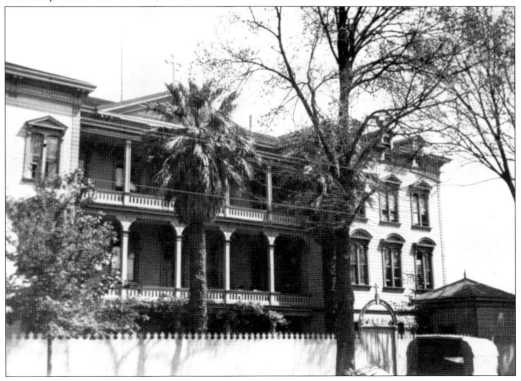

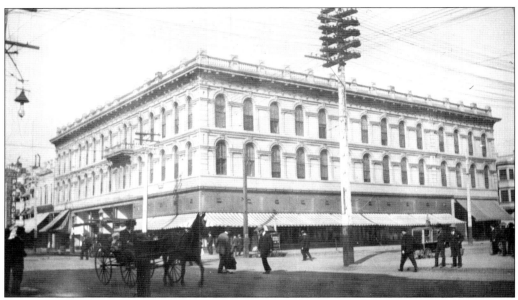

Sacramento's many lodging establishments included the Golden Eagle Hotel, a frequent gathering spot for politicians during the late 1800s. The original 1851 wood structure at 189 K Street was rebuilt in brick in 1853 by Daniel Callahan. By 1867, the hotel welcomed guests at the corner of Seventh and K Streets, including visiting former president Ulysses Grant in 1879. Nearby, the Pantages Theater at 615 K Street is visible at far left in 1909.

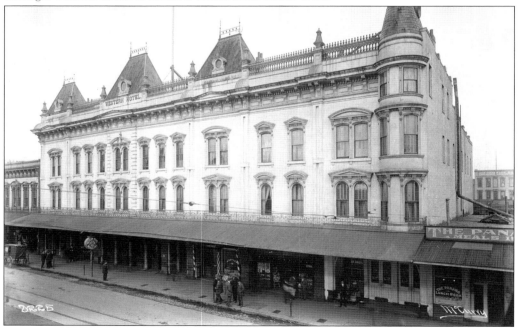

Seen around 1910 is Sacramento's Western Hotel at 209 K Street, constructed in 1854. The hotel's omnibus brought travelers to its door from the train depot and ship docks two blocks away. One of the largest hotels in the West, it featured an elevator and other luxuries. Destroyed by fire in 1875, it was rebuilt in brick that year by hotelier William Land. It was razed in 1960. (CSL.)

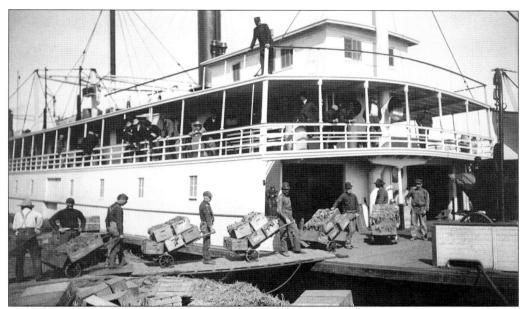

By the early 1900s, Sacramento's dominance as an exporter of flour had weakened due to competition from other American farming regions and falling international prices. Sacramento Valley farmers turned to growing fruits and vegetables, which were shipped to waiting markets by riverboats and railroad cars cooled by ice. Here, the steamboat *Apache*, owned by the Southern Pacific Railroad, is loaded with potatoes while docked in Sacramento around 1910. (CSL.)

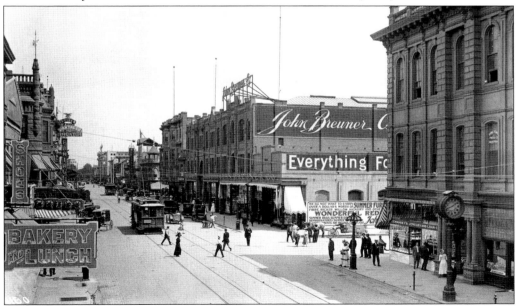

This east-facing view of K Street around 1910 shows a time of transition from horse- to gas-powered transportation. Electric streetcars, horse-drawn carriages, and automobiles are all visible at the corner of K and Sixth Streets. Seen on the far right is the Masonic hall behind a sidewalk clock, and beyond it is John Breuner's furniture company. Other businesses include the Pantages Theater and Golden Eagle Hotel.

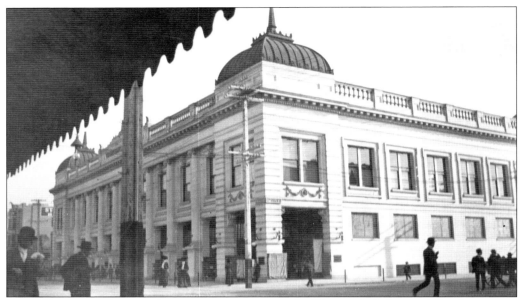

One of Sacramento's iconic shopping institutions was the Weinstock, Lubin, and Co. department store, founded by Harris Weinstock and David Lubin in 1874 at 400 K Street. Leveled by a devastating fire on January 31, 1903, the original structure was replaced at the same location by the "magnificent white building," seen here around 1910. The company moved to its new home at Twelfth and K Streets in 1925.

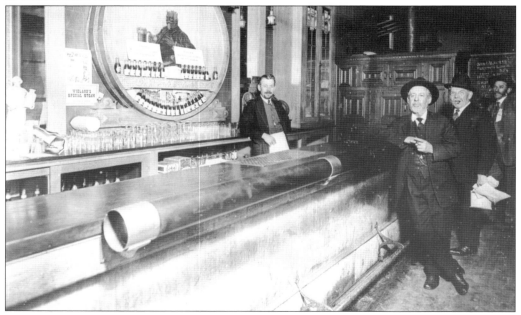

Active since the city's earliest days, Sacramento's German community established the local branch of the Turners, an athletic-social club, by building Turner Hall at 914 K Street in 1859. This c. 1909 photograph shows men in the bar at Turner Hall, which also included a café owned by William Dreher and Louis Graber. This original meeting place of the Turnverein moved to its new home at 3349 J Street in 1925.

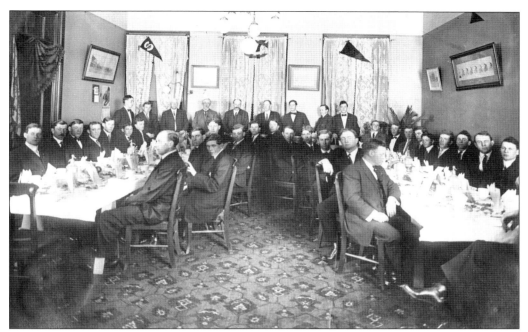

By the late 1800s, bicycling was already a popular activity in Sacramento, leading to the organization of cycling clubs. This 1911 photograph shows a meeting of the Capital City Wheelmen, a bicycle club formed on June 25, 1886. Wheelmen members took part in "club runs" and raced against other cycling groups. In 1896, the Wheelmen provided funds to construct the first bike path connecting Sacramento to Folsom.

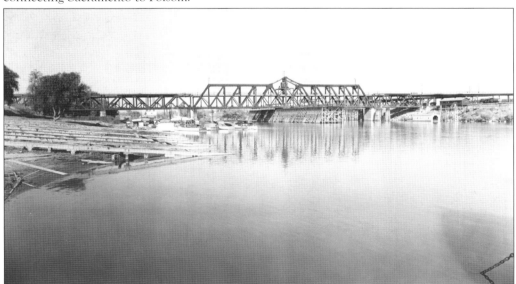

The Southern Pacific Bridge, later called the I Street Bridge and still in use today, was built in 1911 to endure "100 years' service." The fifth bridge built in this location, its predecessors were constructed in 1857, 1870, 1878, and 1895. The bridge's lower span was operated by the railroad, while the upper span served automobiles and pedestrians. Boat launching rails appear on the left in this north-facing 1911 scene.

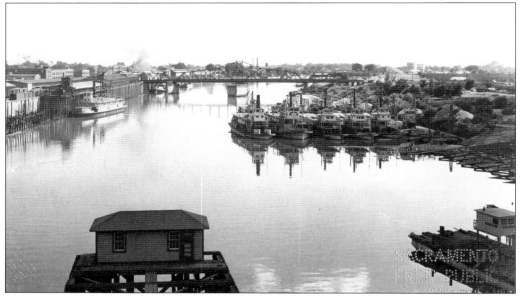

Taken from the I Street Bridge, this c. 1912 photograph gives an expansive view, facing south, of the Sacramento River waterfront and the M Street Bridge. On the right, riverboats are docked along the Broderick section of West Sacramento in Yolo County, while Sacramento's waterfront is seen on the left. Automobiles, pedestrians, and the Northern Electric Railway all used the M Street Bridge, built in 1911.

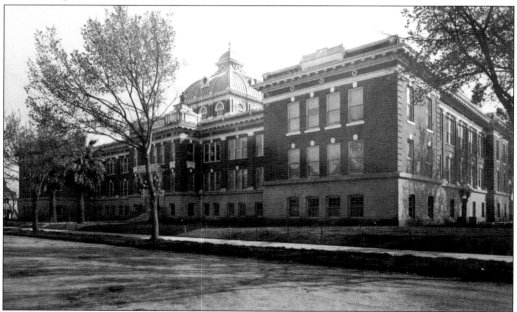

One of the earliest educational institutions in the city was Sacramento High School, seen in this 1912 photograph. While the school originally opened in 1856 at another location, this Georgian-style building was constructed in 1908, designed by architect Rudolph A. Herold and decorated with paintings and statues. In 1924, the high school moved to Thirty-Fourth and W Streets. The pictured structure, located at 1816 K Street, was razed in 1959.

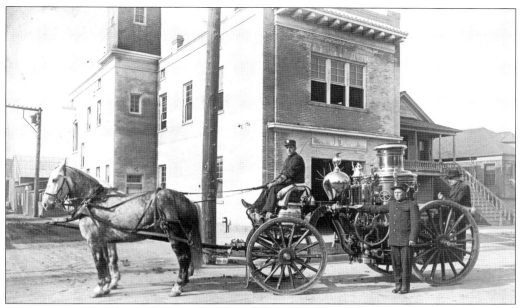

Serving Sacramento since 1850, the all-volunteer Mutual Hook and Ladder Company No. 1 preceded the paid, professional Sacramento Fire Department, which was established in 1872. During the early 1900s, improvements were made in firefighting equipment, and motorized vehicles replaced horse-drawn carriages. In this c. 1915 photograph, three men pose with an engine in front of Engine Company No. 5 Firehouse on Ninth Street between T and U Streets. (CSL.)

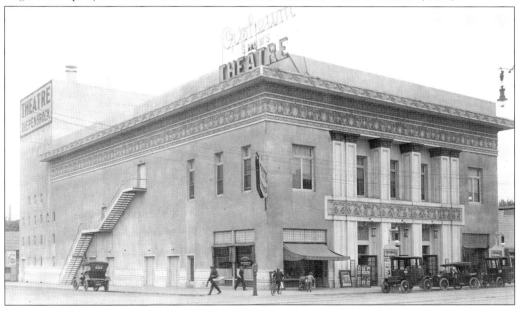

The Diepenbrock Theater, seen in this c. 1913 photograph at 1203 J Street, was named after its founder and owner, German-born Melchior Diepenbrock. Audiences were drawn to vaudeville shows from the Orpheum Circuit that were performed here, as indicated by the sign atop the building which reads, "Orpheum Shows Theatre." The Diepenbrock Theater opened in 1911, became the Strand in 1915, and in 1923 was renamed Loew's State Theater.

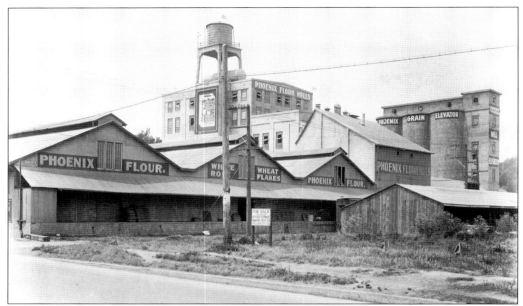

As steamships and the railroad connected Sacramento to the world and made shipping more affordable, agriculture replaced mining as a mainstay of the local economy. One of several flour mills to thrive in Sacramento at this time was the Phoenix Milling Company, established at Thirteenth and J Streets in 1853. Pictured around 1914 at Twelfth and C Streets, the business was sold to the Globe Milling Company in 1928. (CSL.)

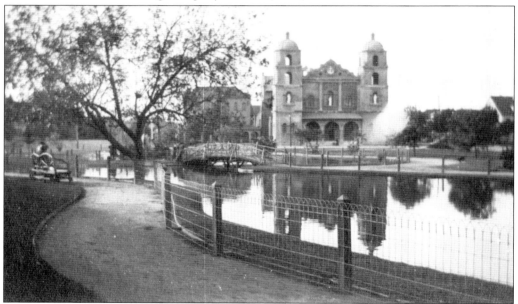

In the late 1800s, Sacramento's expanding population shifted into areas such as Midtown, located between Sixteenth and Thirty-First Streets. Midtown's places of worship included St. Francis Catholic Church, built in 1895 at Twenty-Sixth and K Streets. In 1910, the original structure was replaced by the church seen in this 1913 view from Sutter's Fort. This new church was modeled after the Old Mission Santa Barbara in Santa Barbara, California.

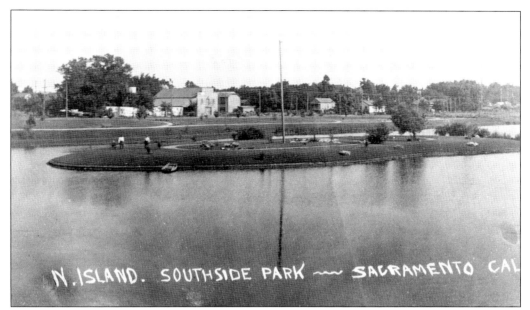

An oasis near Sacramento's center, Southside Park was originally bordered by Sixth, Eighth, T, and X Streets. Prompted by the Southside Improvement Club, the city purchased the property for the future park in 1906 and later transformed its slough into a lake. By the time of this c. 1913 photograph, tennis courts and picnic areas had been added. In 1911, the park hosted a water carnival featuring boat races. (CSH.)

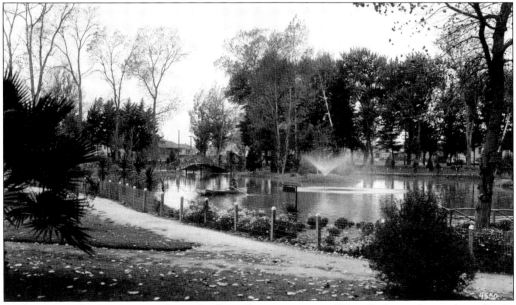

In the 1870s, the Sacramento Street Railway Company opened East Park, just beyond city limits at Thirty-First and H Streets, as an attraction at the end of its trolley line. In 1902, when rail service to the park was discontinued, members of Sacramento's Tuesday Club convinced the city to purchase the land to preserve this community treasure. Seen here around 1915, it was renamed McKinley Park, honoring Pres. William McKinley. (CSL.)

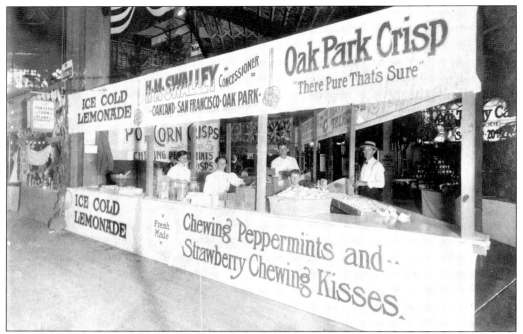

One of Sacramento's major attractions, bringing visitors from throughout the valley, was the popular Joyland amusement park. Located in the streetcar suburb of Oak Park southeast of the city, Joyland featured a roller coaster, swimming pool, tunnel of love, and a small zoo. The concession stands, shown around 1914, were located in the roller-skating rink. Joyland closed in 1927, soon to become the site of McClatchy Park. (CSH.)

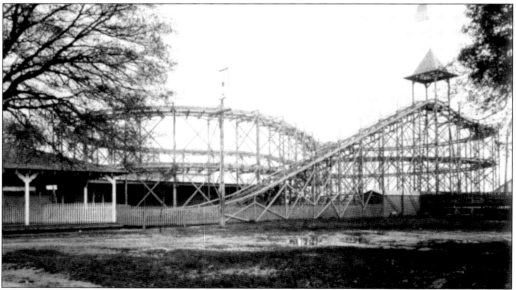

Joyland opened in 1914 at the former location of the Oak Park Amusement Park. This photograph shows one of the park's popular attractions, the Scenic Railway, designed in the early figure-eight style. The Scenic Railway was later torn down and replaced by the Giant Racer roller coaster. In 1920, a fire at Joyland caused $100,000 in damage, destroying part of the Giant Racer. (CSH.)

After Sacramento's city offices relocated from the waterworks building at Front and I Streets to an interim location at 426 J Street, the spacious, New Beaux-Arts city hall was built at 915 I Street. The five-story, 267,000-square-foot building, featuring a tower with four clocks, was designed by prominent local architect Rudolph A. Herold. Opened in 1911, it is seen here around 1915 decorated with flags. (CSL.)

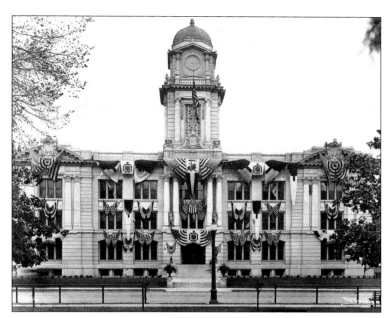

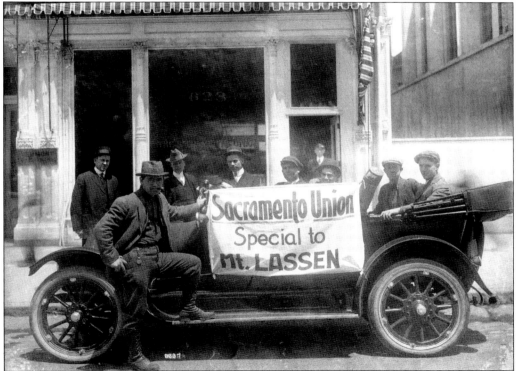

Pausing on May 24, 1915, before embarking on an adventure to observe the erupting Mount Lassen are Harry Spears (front), Darwin J. Smith, J.B. Hoardon, and Harley Frederick. A reporter for the *Sacramento Union*, Smith wrote articles for the newspaper describing the hazardous road conditions and the dependable performance of their Overland Model 81 vehicle. In the background is the *Sacramento Union* office at 623 I Street. (CSL.)

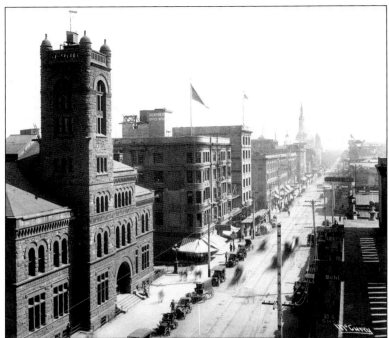

Looking east from Seventh Street, this 1915 view of K Street shows a blur of activity. On the left is Sacramento's red sandstone post office, opened in 1894 on the former site of St. Rose of Lima Catholic Church. The Romanesque Revival building was nicknamed "the pink post office" and was demolished in 1967. Also visible are the Ochsner Office Building and the Cathedral of the Blessed Sacrament. (CSL.)

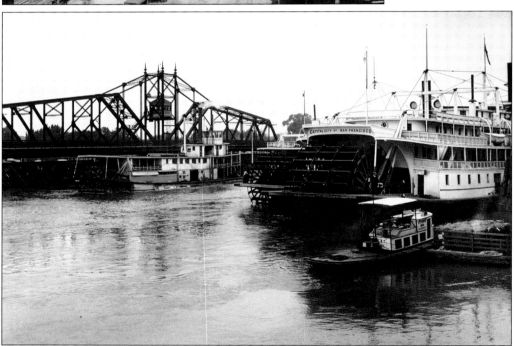

Seen near the M Street Bridge on the Sacramento River in 1915 are, from left to right, the steamboats *Flora*, *Pride of the River*, and *Capital City*, with a tugboat in the foreground. The elegant, four-deck *Capital City* carried passengers on the Sacramento River between Sacramento and San Francisco from 1910 until 1927, when the steamers *Delta King* and *Delta Queen* initiated passenger service on the same route. (CSL.)

Three

The Emergence of a Modern City
1916 to 1945

The ramifications of World War I were felt throughout Sacramento. The people of the Capital City responded to the call of duty by rolling bandages for the Red Cross, planting home gardens, and raising money through Liberty Bond drives. While citizens were hard at work supporting the troops, a great deal of change was also taking place in Sacramento. The completion of the Yolo Causeway marked a period of road and infrastructure improvements designed to accommodate the expanding city. In April 1918, the new Sacramento Public Library opened and began serving approximately 67,000 residents in the city. This era of growth continued into the 1920s.

Postwar Sacramento experienced a time of rapid development and a faster pace of life. Automobiles replaced horse-drawn wagons, and large office buildings were erected on J, K, and L Streets. Memorial Auditorium opened in 1927 and hosted a plethora of events including boxing matches, concerts, and dances. Not only were the 1920s a period of infrastructure growth, the decade was also a time of cultural evolution. Although Sacramento had many theaters before the 1920s, most were venues for silent films. This changed with the advent of the Fox Senator and the Hippodrome, both built by major Hollywood studios. Many, however, would come to believe—and with ample reason—that the finest theater in the city was the Alhambra Theatre.

The Great Depression gripped Sacramento just like it did the rest of the nation; however, the effects were a little delayed in the Sacramento Valley because of a somewhat robust agriculture industry. In a matter of years, shantytowns, or "Hoovervilles" sprouted up along the Sacramento and American Rivers just north of the city. Even with Sacramento's agriculture and canning industries, there were many unemployed and itinerant homeless throughout the city. The implementation of the New Deal brought numerous Works Progress Administration (WPA) projects to Sacramento, including the Tower Bridge, C.K. McClatchy High School, the Overhead Water Tank, the Sacramento Junior College annex and extensions, and the Sacramento City Hall annex. As the country struggled with the Depression, a new challenge threatened the nation.

World War II permanently changed the Sacramento community. After the attack on Pearl Harbor by Imperial Japanese forces, fear and xenophobia drove the decision to incarcerate Japanese Americans. Sacramento's Walerga Assembly Center served as a makeshift detention center for many citizens from throughout Sacramento County.

—Ignacio Sanchez Alonso

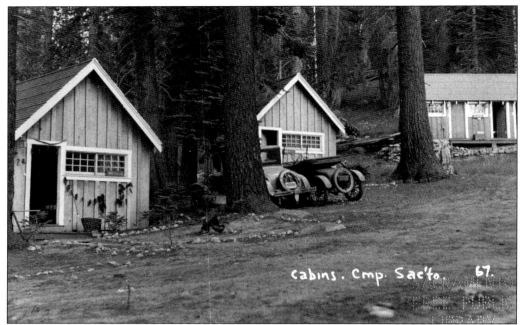

Camp Sacramento opened in 1920 and was located 85 miles east of the Capital City in El Dorado National Forest. The goal of the city-owned camp was to give Sacramento residents an affordable mountain vacation. The campsite was located on 40 acres of mountainous land and featured 36 cabins, a dining hall, laundry services, a store, and library.

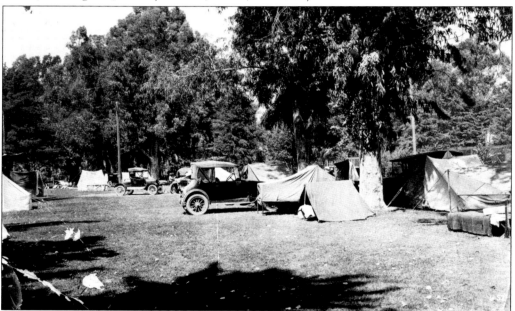

This photograph shows auto camping in Sacramento, but the location of the camp is unknown. As Americans became more mobile, auto camps increased in popularity, offering modern amenities like running water, electricity, and mattress rentals. Many Americans took advantage of the mobility they gained with the advent of automobiles and flocked to these popular auto camps.

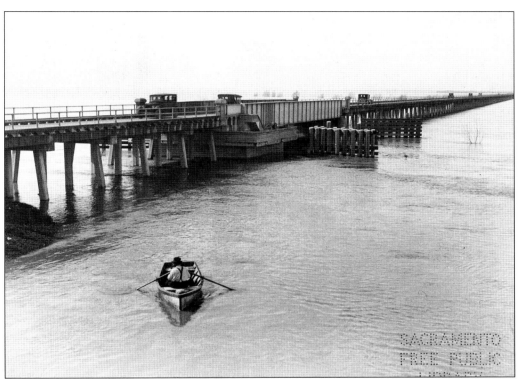

This 1930 photograph shows the Yolo Causeway standing above high water with several vehicles on the roadway. It opened in 1916 and was one of many road improvements designed to make traveling by car easier and faster. During winter months, the bypass would flood, and travelers would have to reroute to Stockton in order to get to Davis or the Bay Area. The causeway made year-round travel possible.

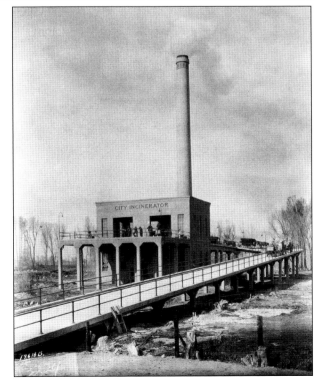

This photograph from 1925 shows the city incinerator. The two-story structure features a chimney and a ramp leading to the second floor. The contract for the construction of the building was awarded to the F.L. DeCarie Company. The incinerator was located north of the B Street levee between Seventh and Ninth Streets. The city purchased the land from the Beatty Estate for $11,000. (CSL.)

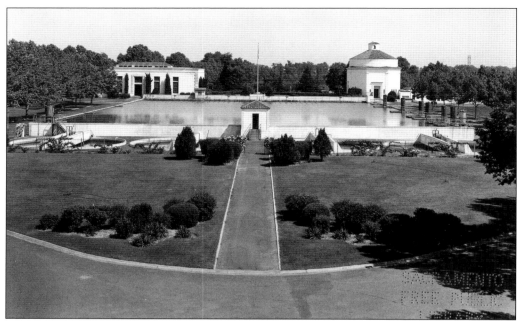

This 1928 photograph shows the Sacramento filtration plant. Built in an Italian Romanesque style, the plant was located just north of the city and the Southern Pacific Railroad yards. The $1,800,000 project was built to furnish the growing city with ample supplies of clean water as well as to provide employment opportunities for Sacramentans.

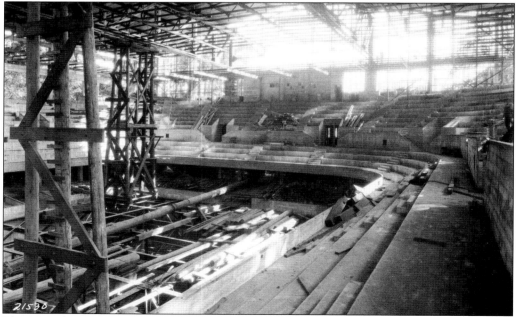

This 1926 photograph shows Memorial Auditorium with interior seating and roof under construction. The edifice featured a particular type of plaster designed to absorb noise. The halls, seating, and roof also featured acoustic plaster. The building contained an abundance of dressing rooms and a tilting floor for theatrical performances. (CSH.)

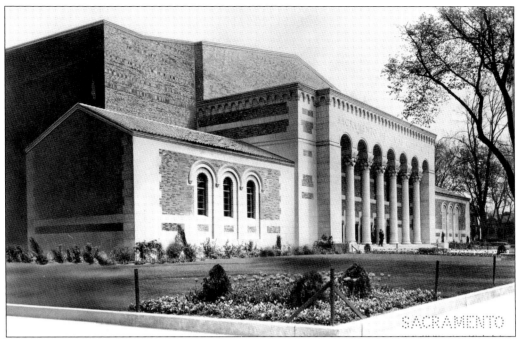

Sacramento's Memorial Auditorium opened its doors to the public in February 1926. The auditorium has continually hosted a variety of professional events, except from 1986 to 1996, when it was closed because it did not meet earthquake safety standards. The Byzantine-style building, as characterized by city architect James S. Dean, was dedicated to those who lost their lives in World War I.

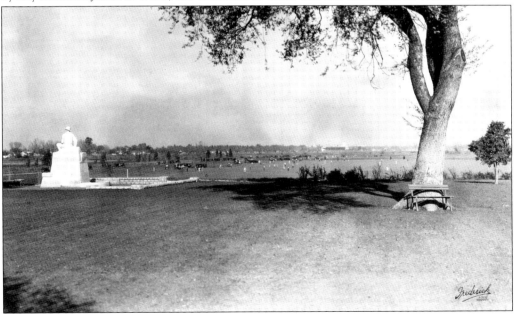

This view of William Land Park is from 1926. The memorial statue and fountain of Charles Swanston are on the left. Ralph Stackpole, the artist commissioned to create the sculpture, also designed the Coleman Fountain in Cesar Chavez Plaza. The state capitol is visible in the distance.

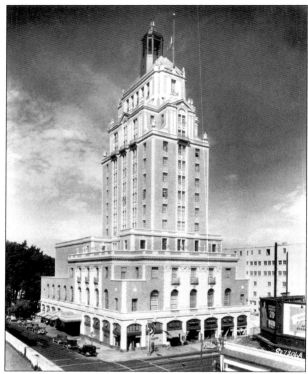

Taken on August 27, 1930, this photograph captures the grandeur of the Elks Tower at Eleventh and J Streets. The construction contract went to the firm of Lindgren and Swinerton, which also worked on the California State Life Insurance Company Building and the Sacramento County Courthouse. Once completed, the building was the tallest in the city at a height of 242 feet.

This photograph, taken June 2, 1937, shows construction at the future site of the American Trust Company. The sign at center reads, "New Bank Building to be erected on this site for the American Trust Company." The structure featured 30-foot ceilings, marble columns, and massive skylights.

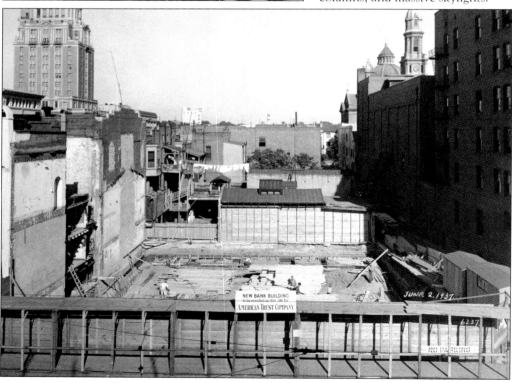

In 1926, New York sculptor Edward Field Sanford Jr. inspects his work on the figures and pediments on the capitol extension buildings. Regarding Sanford's work, Matlack Price, a well-known architectural and sculptural critic, said "he has approached the problem of the pediment with an open mind and a clear eye, giving due recognition to the classical past history of the pediment, but not allowing himself to be intimidated by it."

During the 1920s, Sacramento experienced a period of rapid growth during which K Street flourished and theaters, hotels, restaurants, and shops lined the street. Pictured in 1920 is a parade on K Street. Some businesses include Chinn-Beretta Optical Company (901 K Street), Purnell's Stationery (915 K Street), Hotel Clunie (805 K Street), Hale Bros. department store (825 K Street), and the Sequoia Hotel (911 K Street).

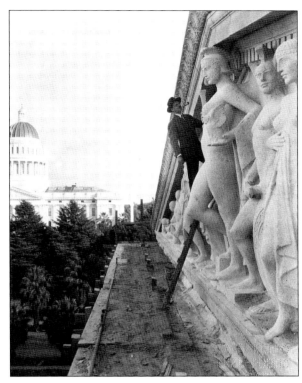

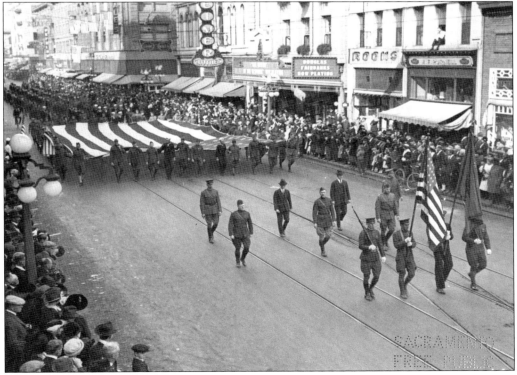

75

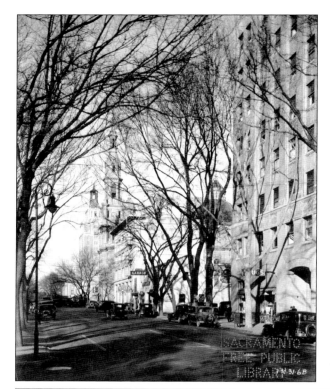

This photograph of Eleventh and K Streets was taken in 1931, showing Casey's Drugs, Dalma Garage, Pacific Gas and Electric, and the Medical Dental Building. The Elks Tower and the Cathedral of the Blessed Sacrament are prominent in the background.

This aerial view of Sacramento around 1930 looks east toward downtown. Some of the prominent structures are the capitol, the new library and court buildings, the California Western State Life Insurance Building, and the Elks Tower. Also worth noting is the Japanese American neighborhood at center. After World War II's internment policy and the construction of Capitol Mall, the neighborhood was erased from downtown.

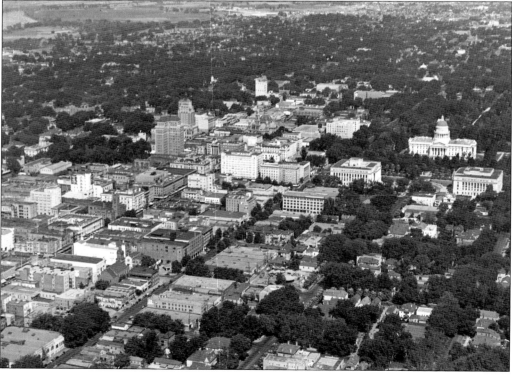

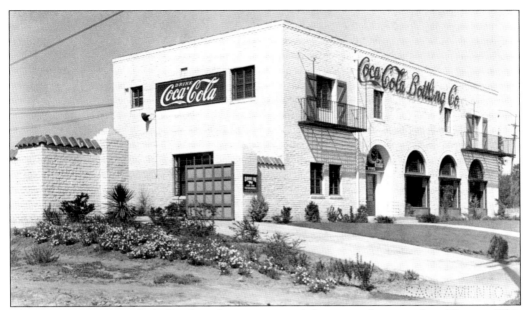

The Sacramento Coca-Cola Bottling Company served the region for more than 77 years. This photograph shows the building as it was in 1936 at its location at 2200 Stockton Boulevard. Nathan M. Sellers acquired the rights to sell Coca-Cola in 1927 and started the company. (CSL.)

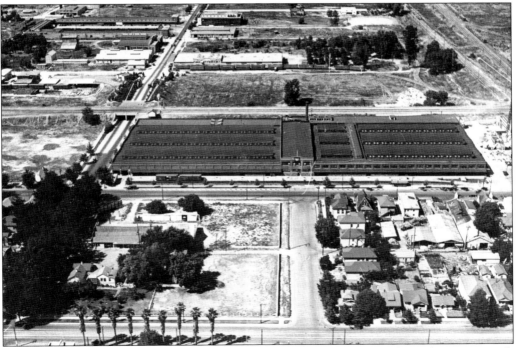

This 1930 aerial view shows the California Packing Corporation Plant No. 11, located at Seventeenth and C Streets. The photograph shows fields, residential buildings, and boxcars. The California Packing Corporation, also known as Calpak, was founded in 1916 by a merger of five different canning operations, which effectively gave Calpak control of California's canning industry.

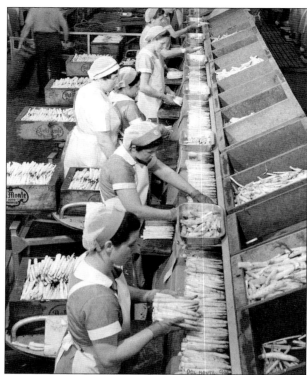

This photograph, taken in 1943, shows a line of cannery workers cleaning, cutting, and preparing white asparagus for canning at the California Packing Corporation. Note the Del Monte asparagus crates. The Del Monte label was reserved for products of the highest quality. (CSH.)

Seen here is the interior of Dr. Henry Yee's herb shop at 707 J Street. Yee arrived in Sacramento in 1906 after receiving a master's degree in engineering from the University of Michigan. After spending time in China working on various engineering projects, he returned to Sacramento in 1930 and established his medical practice. Yee also founded and served as president to the Yee Family Association.

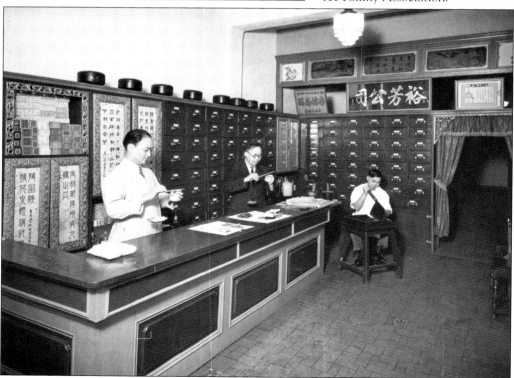

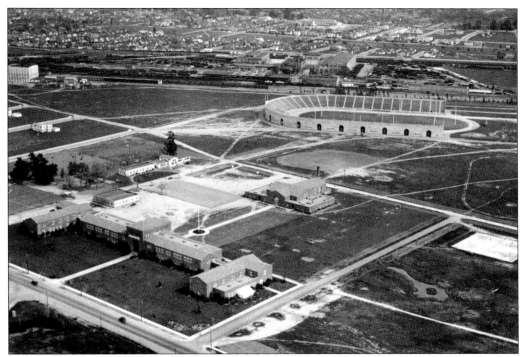

This aerial photograph from 1931 shows Sacramento Junior College. Municipal Stadium is prominent in the background. The college was founded in 1916 by Sacramento High School teacher Belle Cooledge, who was appointed dean of the school in 1920. (CSH.)

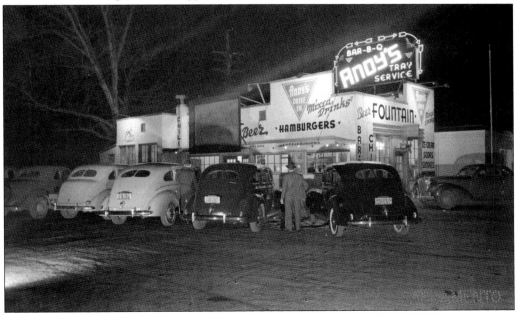

This photograph, taken on the night of February 17, 1939, shows Andy's Bar-B-Q restaurant on North Sixteenth Street. The restaurant's second location was on Freeport Boulevard. The busy drive-in is surrounded by cars and customers.

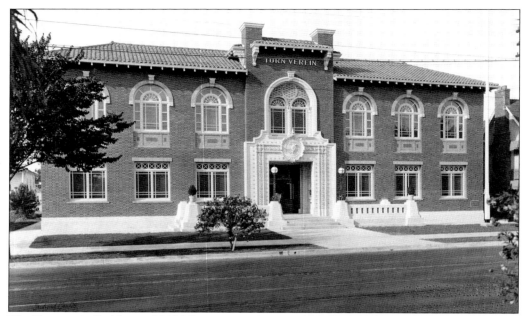

The Turnverein Building at 3349 J Street is seen here in 1925, the year the structure was built. Once completed, the organization moved from its previous location at Ninth and K Streets. The Turnverein was first established in Sacramento in 1854 as a social outlet for the city's German population.

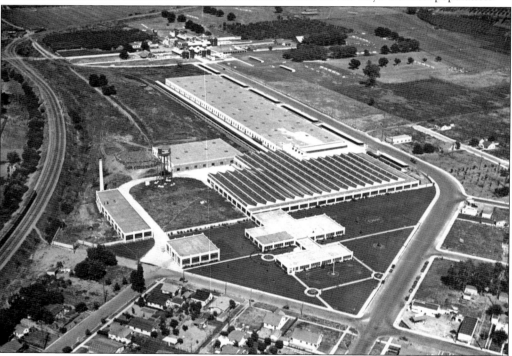

The American Can Company, located at Thirty-Third and C Streets, was a massive complex. This photograph from 1940 shows the size of the compound. Railroad tracks are visible on the left at the levee. The company provided jobs for 900 workers during the summer months. (CSL.)

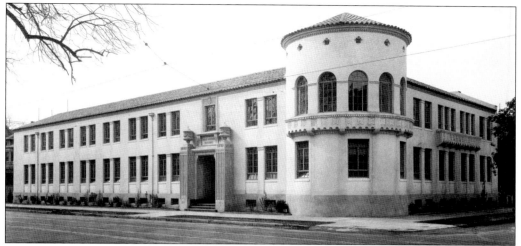

The California Fruit Exchange Building on Tenth Street is captured in this 1934 photograph. The Spanish Revival–style structure was designed by the firm of Starks and Flanders. Opening in 1932, it was occupied by the California Fruit Exchange Company until 1966. The entrance to the left of the tower reads, "Blue Anchor Building." The blue anchor was the emblem of the California Fruit Exchange Company. (CSL.)

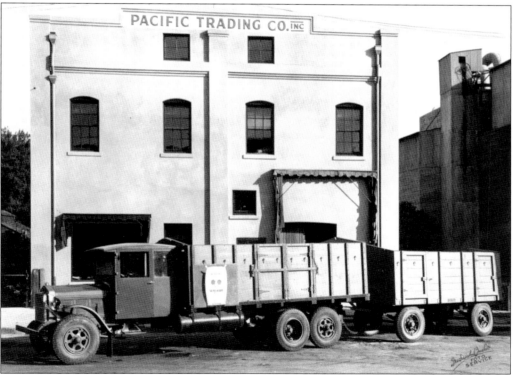

This photograph shows the Pacific Trading Company at its 1515 Front Street location. The company, part of Sacramento's rice industry, partnered with three other local mills, including the California Rice Milling Company, the Garvey-Fiock Milling Company, and the Phillips Milling Company. The placard on the truck reads, "Japan Rice Suyehiro."

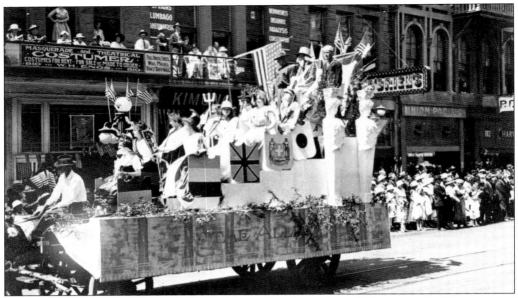

The description on this photograph of a Liberty Bond parade on K Street reads, "Two views of the Washington, Yolo County float in the Liberty Bond Parade, World War I. Girl, second right side from bottom is Kate Williams with Blair M., a soldier air cadet from Mather Field, as Uncle Sam. The sailor was from Mare Island, Vallejo, California." Liberty Bond drives raised more than $30 million. (CSH.)

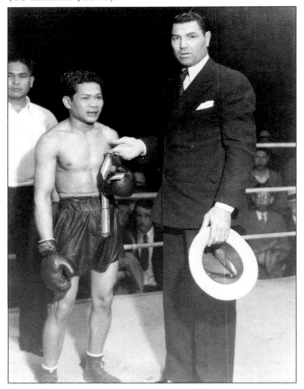

Fernando "Young Tommy" Opao is shown receiving the state bantamweight championship from ex-heavyweight champion Jack Dempsey. Opao pummeled "News Boy" Brown, with all 10 rounds going to the Filipino star. The fight took place on the evening of January 28, 1932, in front of a sold-out crowd at Memorial Auditorium.

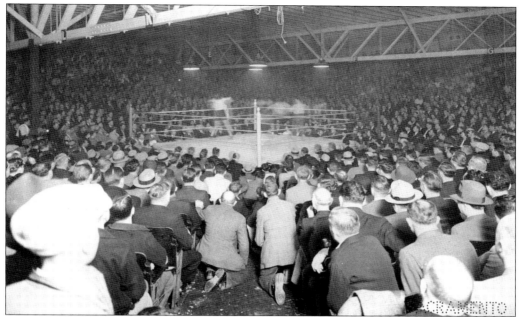

The L Street Arena hosted many sporting events, including boxing, jiu-jitsu, and wrestling. On the evening of November 22, 1935, the overcrowded arena hosted a bout between heavyweight champion James Braddock and sparring partner Jack McCarthy. Sacramento resident and former champion Max Baer was present, but did not partake in any of the bouts.

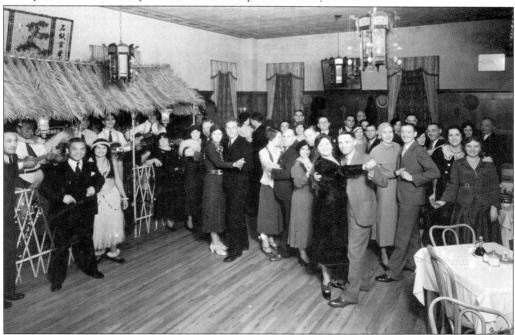

Numerous patrons gathered on October 13, 1932, to help the Hong King Lum Café celebrate its second anniversary at its new location on 304 I Street. The proprietors of the restaurant spared no expense and hired Prince Kawelo and his group of entertainers. The musicians are on the left.

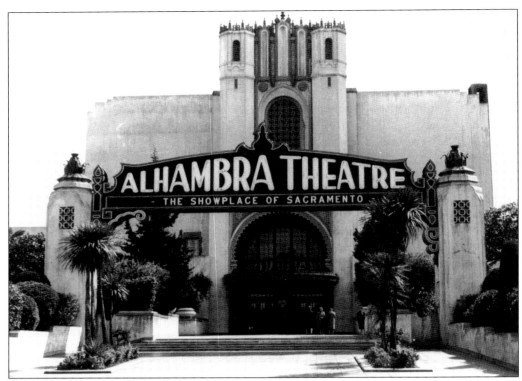

During its prime, the Alhambra Theatre was the most beloved movie house in Sacramento. Its architecture was modeled after the world-famous castle in Granada, Spain, including Moorish-style arches, gardens, and a courtyard and fountain. A host of civic leaders and Hollywood celebrities attended the grand opening celebration on September 24, 1927.

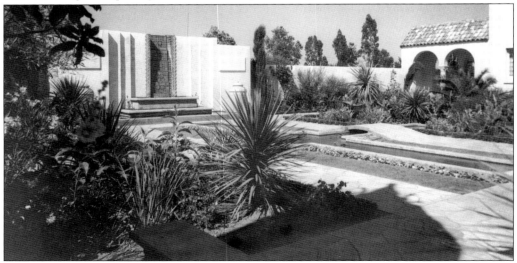

This 1929 photograph shows the lavish courtyard and fountain of the Alhambra Theatre. Located on the back of the theater, the courtyard stayed true to the style of Moorish Spain. The modern building featured seating for up to 2,000 guests—1,600 in the auditorium and 400 in the gallery. The fountain in the background is the only surviving feature of the luxurious theater. (CSH.)

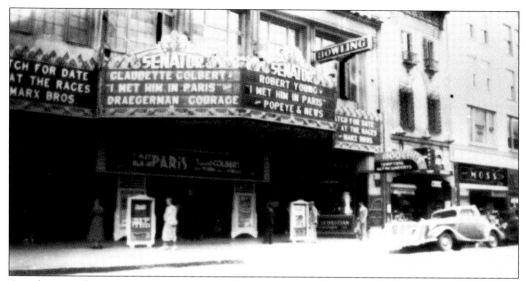

Another popular entertainment venue of the time was the Fox Senator Theatre on K Street. The marquee advertises the movie *I Met Him in Paris*, a romantic comedy starring Claudette Colbert and Robert Young. There is a sign above the marquee for the Crown Bowling Alley, located above the theater. (CSH.)

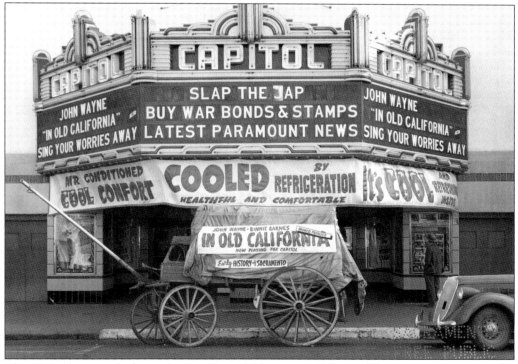

This 1942 photograph shows the Fox Capitol Theatre on K Street. The marquee promotes the Western movie *In Old California* starring John Wayne. As a sign of much different times, the marquee reads, "Slap the Jap Buy War Bonds & Stamps." Signs below the marquee also advertise air-conditioned theater rooms. The wagon parked in front was a prop for the movie.

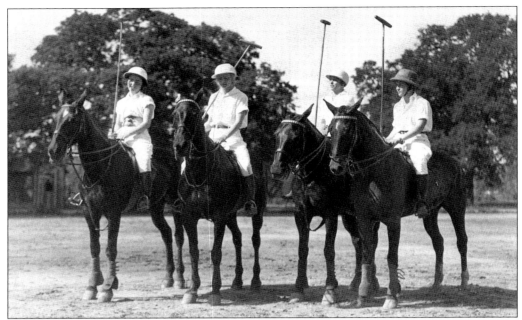

Four female polo players pose with mallets in hand. Polo received an increase in public recognition with the construction of a polo field in the interior of the track at the California State Fairgrounds. This photograph was taken in 1930 at the Sacramento Riding Club field in the Del Paso district of Sacramento County.

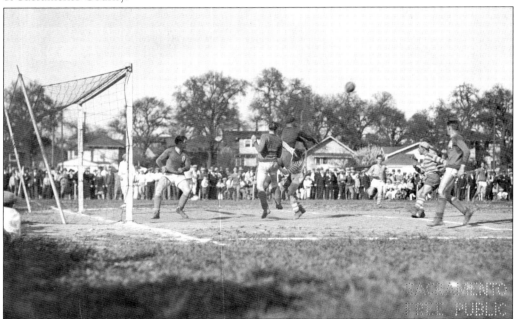

This c. 1930 photograph shows a soccer game between the Western Pacifics (striped uniforms) and the De Molays at Western Pacific Field. Players are scrambling to intercept a cross. During the 1930s, the Sacramento Soccer League included the Western Pacifics, Garibaldis, Dantes, Caledonians, and Celtics. The neighborhood in the background is Curtis Park.

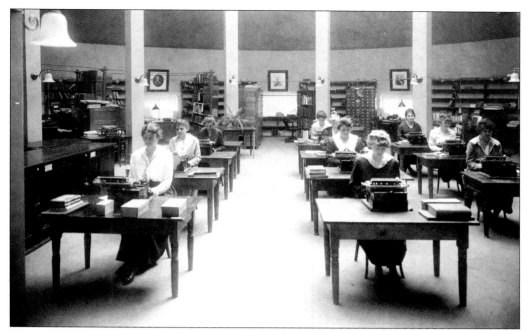

This 1919 photograph captures a group of women who were part of the California State Library's library school and training program. This particular class was held at the capitol, since the library did not move out of the capitol until 1928, when the library annex building was completed. (CSL.)

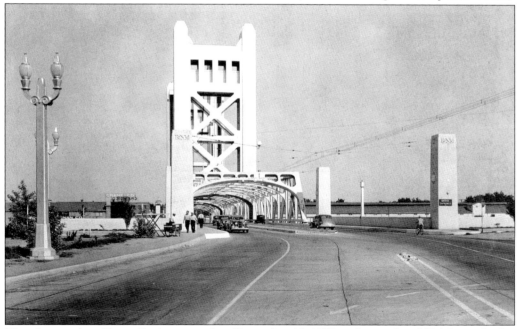

The ultra-modern Tower Bridge opened on December 15, 1935, replacing the old M Street Bridge constructed by the Northern Railway Company in 1910. Increases in population and traffic made the old bridge inadequate and dangerous. The WPA-funded bridge was built by the state Department of Public Works in cooperation with the City and County of Sacramento.

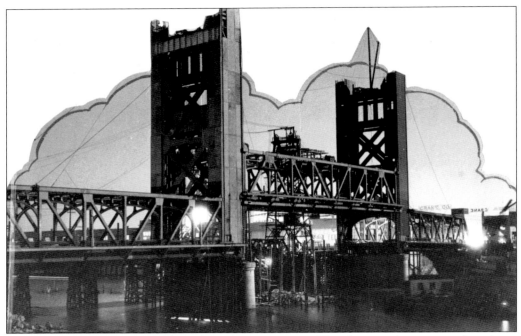

The Tower Bridge is shown midway through construction. The photograph appears to have been taken at night. There is a crane working on the center lift portion of the bridge, and the two 160-foot towers are close to completion. The Tower Bridge added two sidewalks for pedestrians and was wide enough to support modern vehicles. (CSH.)

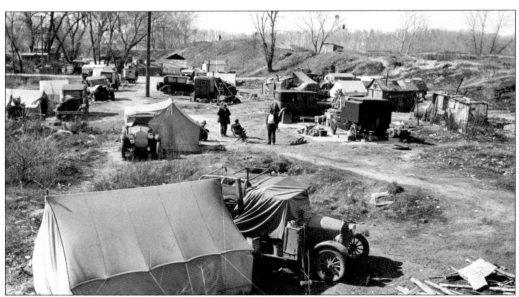

This photograph, dated March 4, 1933, shows a shantytown, or "Hooverville" near the American River. The Great Depression forced many homeless people to take refuge in makeshift dwellings along the American and Sacramento Rivers. These settlements lacked access to clean water and posed major health risks, especially during the rainy season. (CSH.)

This 1940 photograph shows one of Sacramento's three elevated, reinforced concrete water tanks. At the time of their completion, they were some of largest ever constructed. Each had a capacity of three million gallons. Partly funded by the WPA, the Alhambra Reservoir tank provided water to a large part of East Sacramento. The structure has also served as a blood bank and public art canvas. (CSL.)

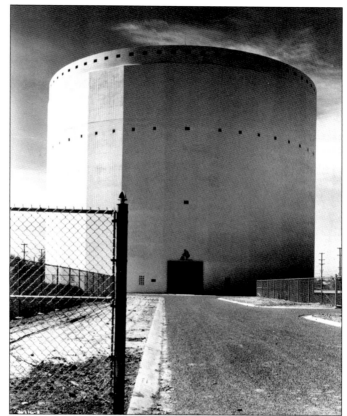

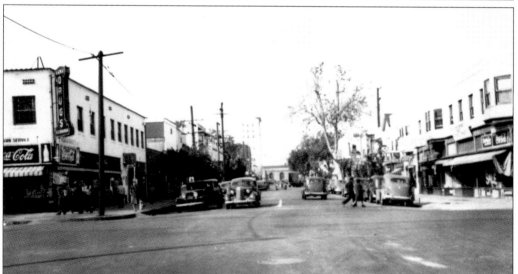

The Japanese American commercial district, known more popularly as Japan Town, is seen here looking north at the intersection of Fourth and M Streets. The photograph was taken in 1942, just before the internment of the Japanese American community. The area would eventually be razed and turned into the Capitol Mall. (CSH.)

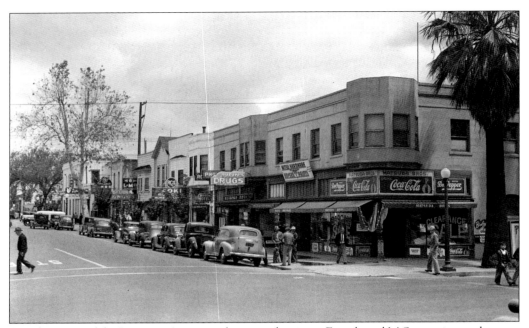

Another view of the Japanese American business district at Fourth and M Streets is seen here on May 11, 1942, a few days before relocation. Businesses include Matsuda Bros., Mitsu Hardware, Suzuki's Drugs, Nippon Hotel, and Kuroko Foto. The neighborhood never recovered from the forced exodus of its residents. (NARA.)

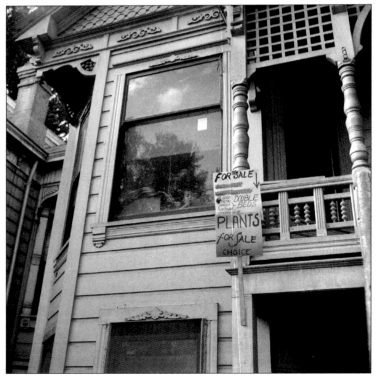

Japanese American citizens were not permitted to take more than a few things with them to relocation centers. Some of the lucky ones left their belongings with neighbors, but most had to sell what they could not take. This photograph, taken May 11, 1942, shows a home with a sign on the balcony advertising beds and plants for sale. There is a child in the window to the left of the sign. (NARA.)

A Japanese American family arrives at the Walerga Detention Center north of Sacramento on May 20, 1942. Prior to being assigned a barracks, they would be registered and medically examined, while their baggage was inspected for contraband. The hastiness in which the detention center was created is evident in the crudeness of the barracks. (NARA.)

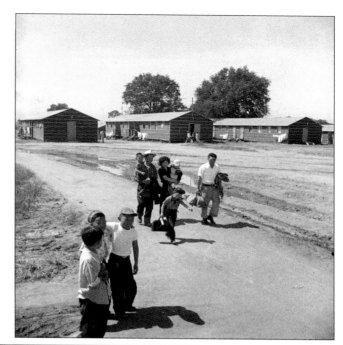

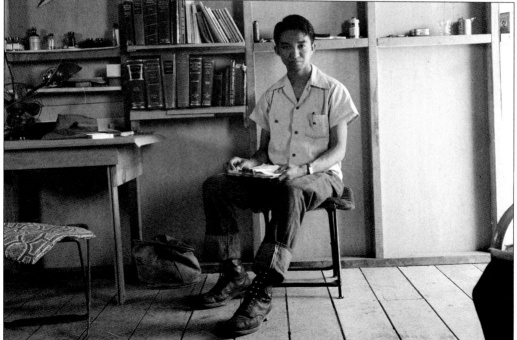

Harvey Akio Itano is pictured here inside his barracks at Walerga. Itano received a bachelor of science in chemistry from the University of California, Berkeley, but was unable to attend commencement ceremonies because of having to report to the detention center. During graduation, university president Robert Gordon Sproul said about him, "He cannot be here with us today. His country has called him elsewhere." (NARA.)

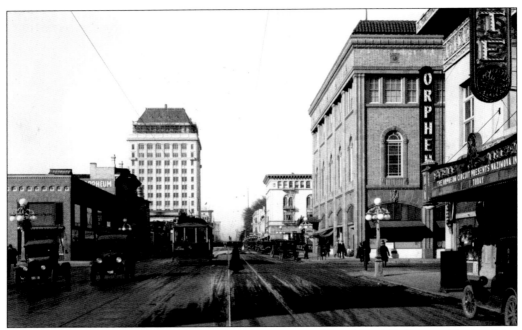

This 1924 photograph captures the bustling intersection of J and Twelfth Streets. To the right, the State Theatre marquee announces its latest matinee. Adjacent to the theater is the Bank of Sacramento. The trolley car in the center is No. 24, and the destination sign reads, "Jst Oak Park." The California State Life Insurance Company Building is prominent in the background. (CSH.)

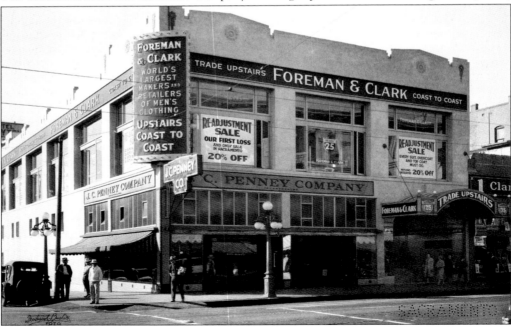

Seen on October 30, 1930, is the Foreman & Clark clothing store and the J.C. Penney store on K Street. Foreman & Clark was on the upper floor, and J.C. Penney was on the first. Foreman & Clark opened in May 1930 and offered costumers over 6,000 garments to choose from.

Four

A FUTURE OF OPTIMISM AND TUMULT
1946 TO PRESENT

World War II had an unalterable impact on the Sacramento region. Powered through the presence of McClellan and Mather Air Force Bases and the Sacramento Army Depot, plus a multitude of war-industry transplants, the county population surged from 170,000 in 1940 to 580,000 in 1963, while the value of countywide building permits tripled from $48 million in 1952 to $145 million in 1962. In mobilizing for both the Cold War and a future spiked with optimism, the region expanded unlike at any other time in its long history.

The 1940s and 1950s also ushered in a new breed of consumerism. Government-subsidized education for returning service members, increased wages, an easier path to home ownership, and the irresistible appeal of new consumer products geared to provide better living brought Sacramentans into a new era that, in the words of historian Steven Avella, "enshrin[ed] mass consumption as a defining characteristic of U.S. culture." Accordingly, shopping hubs like Town & Country Village and Country Club Centre emerged to meet the demands of the region's hyper-suburbanization as manifested through new neighborhoods like Arden Park Vista and Rosemont. Meanwhile, Sacramento's urban core, once irresistible and culturally vital, faded—with some exceptions—into a sandbox of crude government buildings, redevelopment projects, and blighted slums.

The 1960s witnessed a steady infusion of talent, ethnicity, and race that would come to make Sacramento one of the most culturally vibrant spots in the nation. At the same time, shifting sensibilities, both toward government and the status quo, rang in antiwar and social justice movements. Though not always peaceful, protests sought to bring a dissenting voice to the Vietnam War and the area's growing racial and socioeconomic inequalities.

As the 1970s and 1980s emerged, the indispensability of automobile travel presented city and county officials with the dual challenge of growing an ever-expanding web of freeways while also considering smarter and cleaner ways to deliver area commuters from point A to point B. And with the arrival of the new millennium, a spirited rededication to urban living has stood juxtaposed to the monumental task of finding services and housing for all citizens.

—James C. Scott

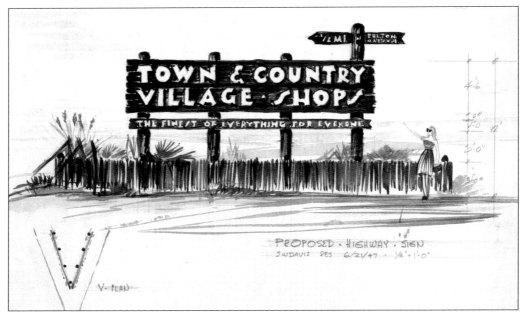

This conceptual drawing was created in June 1947 by John W. Davis, the architectural mind behind the Western-themed Town & Country Village, located at the intersection of Fulton and Marconi Avenues. Opened in 1946 by developer Jere Strizek, the wildly innovative and nationally recognized open-air mall served as a commercial anchor to the quick postwar development of Sacramento's northern suburbs.

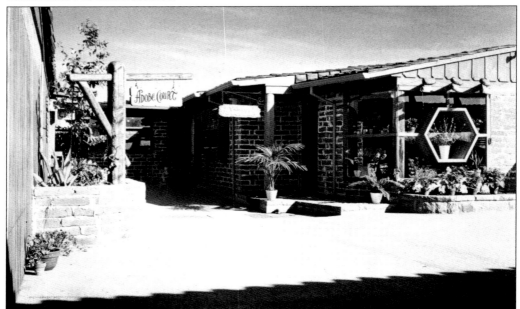

Shown is the Adobe Court portion of Jere Strizek's Town & Country Village. Strizek wanted to break monotony by varying design concepts between the shopping center's numerous sections. Holding much of the experience together, however, was soft music and a rustic Old West–style look by way of bridge timbers salvaged from a defunct railroad line in Sutter County.

The splendor of the newly built Town & Country Village is captured in the neon glow of this c. 1955 image. Billed as the first of its kind in California and covering the equivalent of five city blocks, the shopping center's theme was inspired by developer Jere Strizek's childhood fascination with old California's mission architecture and semitropical flora. The facade of the Village Theater glows at bottom.

Jere Strizek developed Town & Country Village with an eye on having ample consumers nearby to support it. Pictured in 1950 are units of the Village Tract neighborhood, which—along with those in the similar Bohemian Village and Vienna Woods neighborhoods—became known as "Strizek flat tops" because of their flat-style roofs. Strizek contended that "the happiest people in America live right here in these little houses."

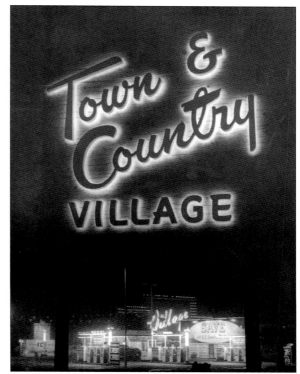

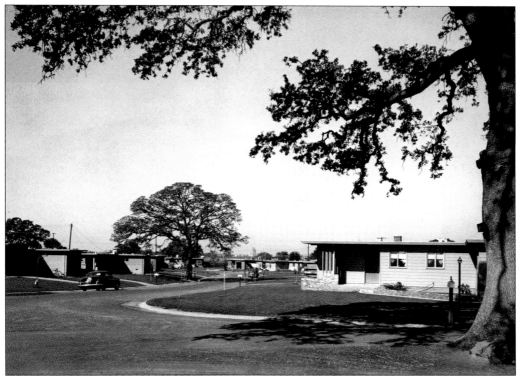

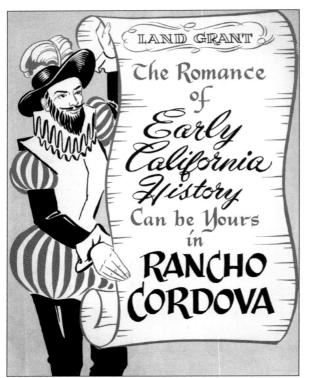

Blending conquistador with Sacramento's Mexican land grant past makes for a flier of kitsch, promoting the real estate–driven community of Rancho Cordova. With the east county's agricultural industries waning and Aerojet and Mather Field rising, vintner Roland Federspiel turned to real estate with his first homes—the ranch-style "Cordovan"—popping up on Zinfandel Drive in November 1953 with a celebratory event emceed by Art Linkletter.

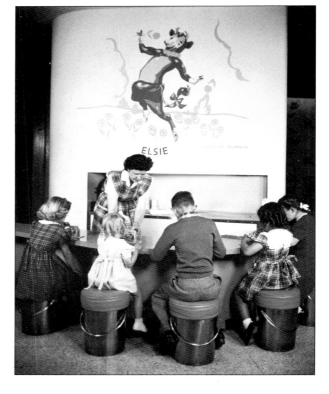

In 1949, contented children drink their milk below the watchful eye of Elsie the Cow at the Weinstock, Lubin, and Co.'s milk bar, a beloved feature of the store's youth center at Twelfth and K Streets. Sacramento-born Nancy Phillips told the Sacramento Public Library in 2009 that the bar "was scaled to us . . . you did not have to have mom and dad there paying for you . . . it was your world." (CSH.)

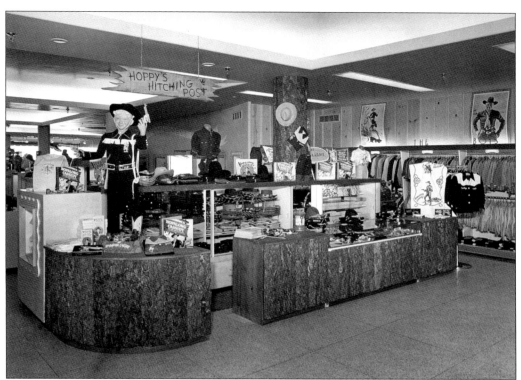

Hoppy's Hitching Post was the subject of this 1950 photograph, taken within the youth center at Weinstock, Lubin, and Co.'s Twelfth and K Streets location. The section offered everything from nickel-plated repeater guns for $1 to deputy hats for $1.95. Young Sacramentans could catch the *Hopalong Cassidy* radio show on KXOA and then KROY or in local theaters like the Liberty, Sequoia, or Del Paso. (CSH.)

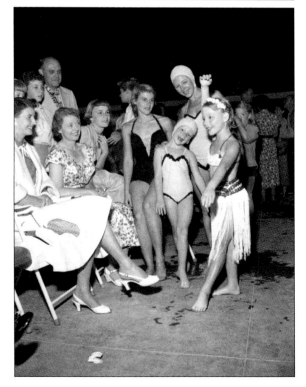

Adoring eyes gaze toward a young swimmer performing the hula during downtime at the Amateur Athletic Association Junior Olympics, held at South Land Park's newly constructed Park Terrace Swimming and Tennis Club in September 1954. Postwar Sacramento grew into a hotbed of swimming talent, producing Olympic gold medalists like Summer Sanders, Mike Burton, Debbie Meyer, Jeff Float, and Mark Spitz. (CSH.)

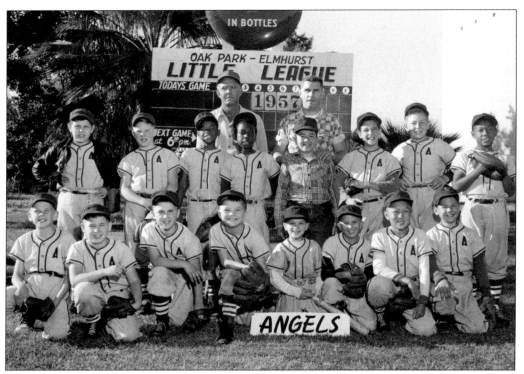

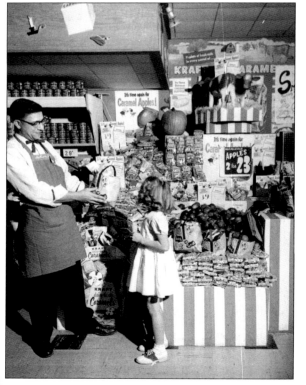

Smiling for the camera at their V Street field in 1957 are the Oak Park–Elmhurst Little League Angels. Sacramento Little League became the city's first youth league in 1952. By 1956, the greater Sacramento area had a total of 22 franchises, from Woodland to Placerville, for 1,500 boys, giving the Sacramento area the second-highest concentration of youth baseball leagues in the nation. Oak Park–Elmhurst received its charter in 1953.

Grocer Al Silva shares a sweet pre-Halloween moment with a young girl at North Highlands' Cardinal grocery store in 1953. A groundswell of supermarkets, including Raley's, Lucky, Cardinal, Inks, Safeway, Bel Air, Stop-N-Shop, and eventually, Cardinal-Inks, were motivated to match and profit from the growth of the city's burgeoning middle class. By 1955, supermarkets were responsible for 60 percent of the groceries sold to Americans. (CSH.)

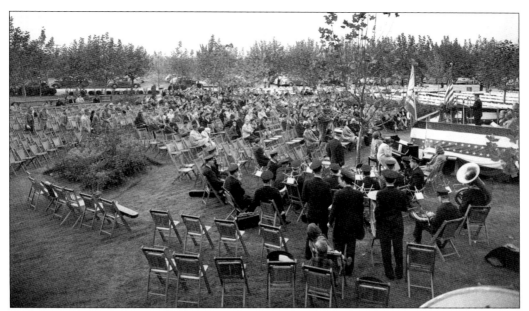

Dedication ceremonies were held in 1949 for Sacramento State College's future campus, a 288-acre swathe along the southern banks of the American River. Known as the White and Terry Tract, it had been the home to orchards, hops fields, and the extinct Gold Rush–era villages of Norristown and Hoboken. Six separate locations were considered for the campus, including the 142-acre Jacinto Tract on Fruitridge Road, east of Stockton Boulevard.

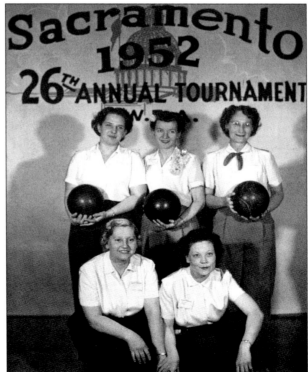

Pictured are participants in the 1952 state women's bowling tournament, which showcased 430 of California's finest female keglers at the Alhambra Bowl. The winning team represented Sacramento's Top of the Town restaurant, occupying the top floor of the Elks Tower. The rise of bowling alleys in the 1950s and 1960s offered a reasonably priced diversion for middle- and lower-class Americans, effectively making bowling alleys "country clubs for the public."

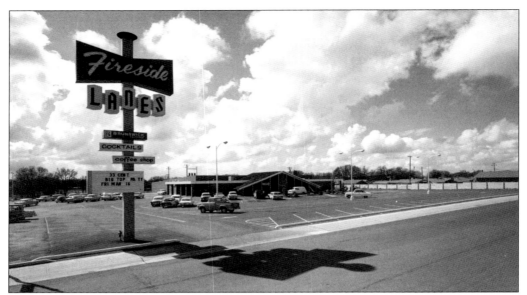

Fireside Lanes bowling alley at 7901 Auburn Boulevard is seen here in 1960. At this time, the Fireside was one of 16 alleys in Sacramento County and one of many built in the "California style," offering opulent lounges, high-beamed ceilings, and flashy external designs. The suburban bowling alley's rise—most of Sacramento's were just that—was aided by automated lanes, eager investors, and a growing middle class.

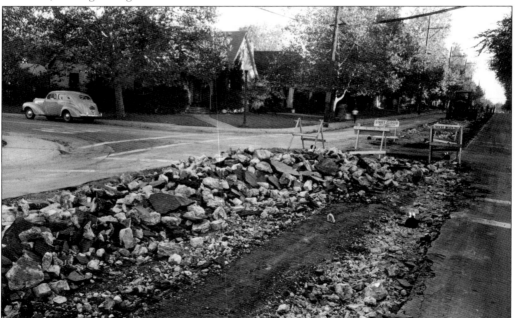

Rails are ripped from a neighborhood street in 1947, part of a citywide conversion from streetcar to bus. Considered by many to be a monumental hassle, the work was done mostly by the city with costs that approached $100,000, all defrayed by Sacramento City Lines, the business with the most to gain in the conversion. The city made considerable money auctioning off the metal rails for roughly $27 a ton. (CSL.)

Shown in 1950 is the entrance to the newly opened Fruitridge Drive-In, located at Fruitridge Road and Stockton Boulevard. The venue featured the largest all-steel screen in Northern California, parking capacity for 850 cars, and a free nursing bottle service. Hometown Lawrence Construction Company and four other local contractors built the complex, which opened on Friday, June 2, 1950, with an 8:00 p.m. showing of *The Third Man*. (CSH.)

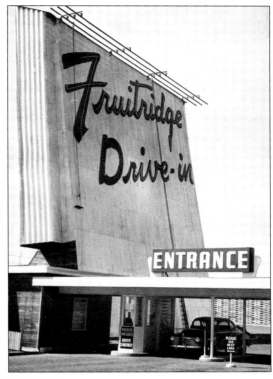

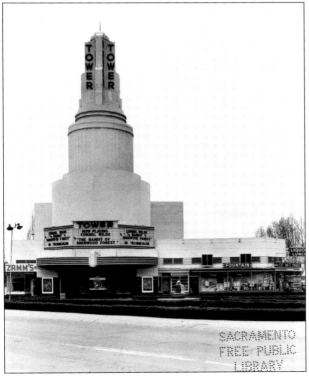

This 1946 image captures an area icon in the Tower Theatre and the birthplace of an international icon in Tower Records. The latter grew out of Clayton Solomon's Tower Cut-Rate Drugs, where, in 1950, son Russ introduced used jukebox 45s to the inventory. By 1960, Tower's fresh new business model promised to keep stores "Open 'til midnite 368 days a year."

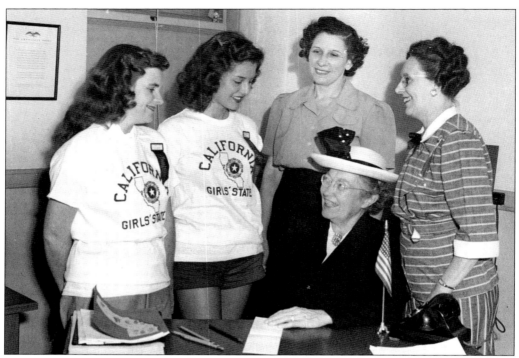

Sacramento mayor Belle Cooledge (seated) gives campaigning advice to Girls' State participants in 1948. The Sutter Creek–born Cooledge was the Capital City's first female mayor, having been appointed to the position in 1948. Beyond serving several years as a member of the Sacramento City Council, she was also a math teacher, founding dean of Sacramento Junior College, and World War I–era nurse.

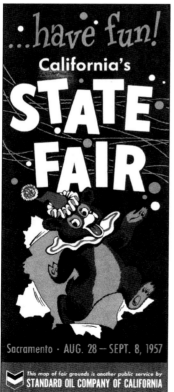

The California bear explodes onto the scene with this 1957 California State Fair and Exposition brochure and map. By the late 1950s, the fair was among the top five largest state fairs in the country, and drew by far the largest attendance of any state fair on the West Coast. It was expanded to 12 days in 1956, drawing nearly 840,000 citizens, with near identical numbers coming in for 1957.

This 1954 California State Fair display represents McClellan Air Force Base's 4701st (then 552nd) Airborne Early Warning and Radar Control squadron. Maid of California Phyllis Yarwood holds a miniature Lockheed EC-121D "Warning Star," a radar-equipped 17-man workhorse and feature of Operation Sentry, an early-warning system on both coasts. The 552nd was one of two Sacramento units to see time in Vietnam, the other being Mather's 320th Bomb Wing. (CSH.)

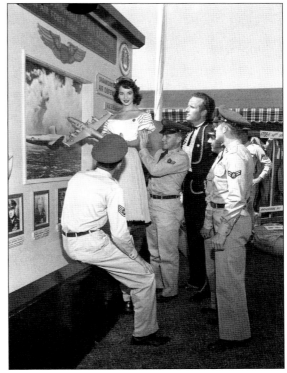

A Sacramento Solons batboy and several recipients of baseballs smile in 1954 at Edmonds Field, located at Broadway and Riverside Boulevard. Edmonds was the Solons' penultimate home, with the team playing out the 1974–1976 seasons at the built-for-football Hughes Stadium, which boasted a bizarrely short 251-foot left field porch. After the Solons, Capital City baseball went into dormancy until the arrival of the Sacramento River Cats in 2000.

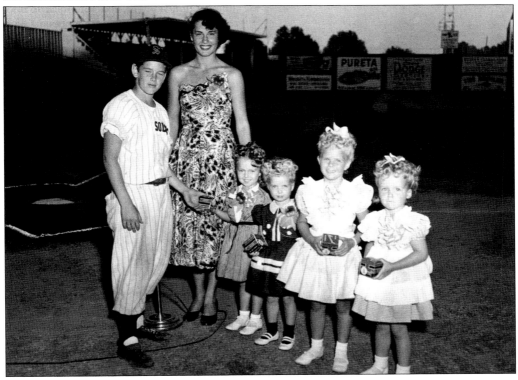

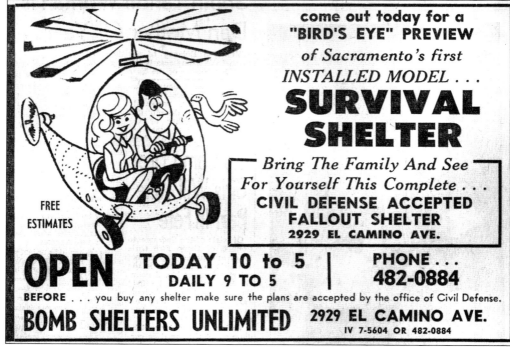

Cold War flashpoints like the Soviet Union's acquisition of nuclear weapons in late 1949 and the shocking launch of *Sputnik* in 1957 sent many Sacramentans into an anxious search for protection from "the bomb." Shown above is a March 1960 advertisement for Bomb Shelters Unlimited. Several local contractors, some licensed, some not, did what they could to leverage popular angst into profit. Government efforts to provide civil defense eventually caught up, as by the time of 1962's Cuban Missile Crisis, Sacramento County offered the relative safety of 47 different fallout shelters for some 97,437 citizens. The image below shows a Sacramento family huddled into their new bomb shelter in 1952. (Both, CSH.)

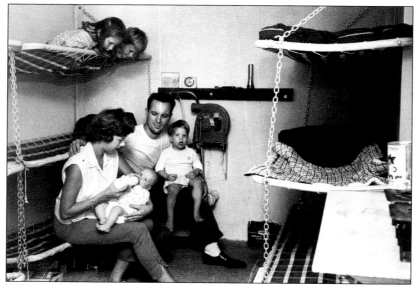

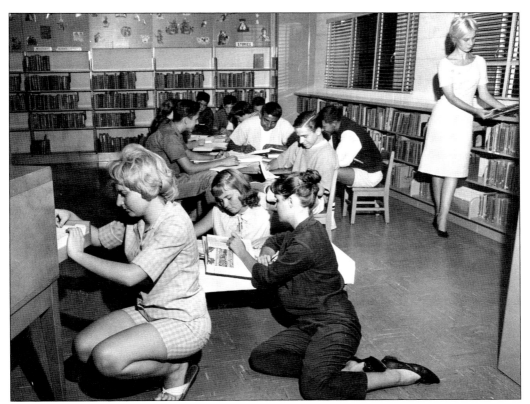

Young readers fill Tahoe Park's Mabel Gillis Branch of the Sacramento City Library in October 1960. Between 1950 and 1960, system-wide circulation nearly doubled from 595,768 to 993,221, due in no small part to the increase in countywide school populations, a growing fascination with science, and a rededication of school curriculums to the topic after the Soviet Union's launch of *Sputnik*.

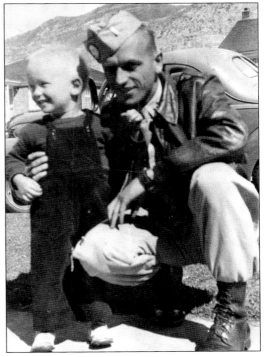

Shown in Utah in 1945 is a tender first meeting between Lt. Robert W. Tribe Sr. and son Robert "Bob" Jr. The elder Tribe was fighting in Europe, where he was wounded three times with the 82nd Airborne. By 1954, the Tribes, including Bob's younger brother Terry and mother, Annette, had settled in Sacramento's Arden-Arcade area, with Robert Sr. working as an engineer for the Bureau of Reclamation. (BT.)

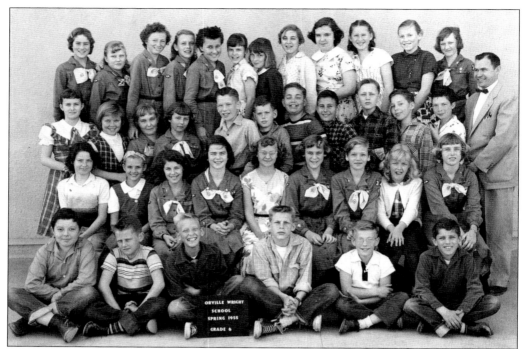

Captured in the spring of 1955 is a joyful Bob Tribe (front row, third from left) along with fellow sixth-graders at Arden Oaks' Orville Wright School. Tribe flourished in the semirural environs of Sacramento's northeastern outskirts, recalling being dropped off by his father at the old Fair Oaks Bridge with a .22-caliber rifle and hunting his way, along with friends, down the American River and back home by day's end. (BT.)

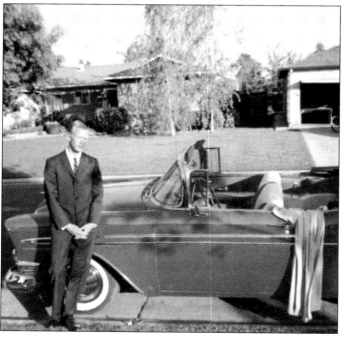

Recently graduated from El Camino High School, Bob Tribe poses with his beloved 1956 Chevy Bel Air convertible in June 1961. He paid for the car by bagging groceries at Mayfair Market and working summers with the Bureau of Reclamation as an engineering aide. Tribe was soon off to San Francisco State College, where he earned a bachelor's degree and later a master's in public administration. (BT.)

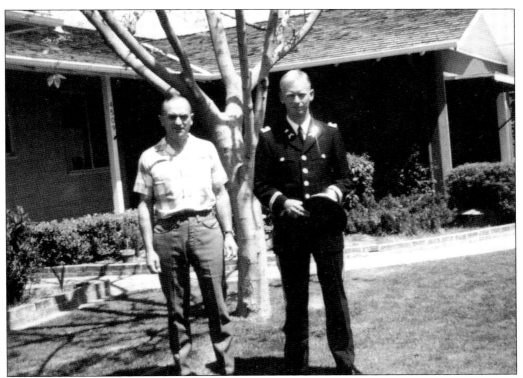

In 1968, father and son stand before their home at 4509 Juno Way. With war raging in Southeast Asia, 1st Lt. Bob Tribe, clad in his Army dress blues, finished Officers' Candidate School at Fort Benning, Georgia. After completing jungle-warfare training in northwestern Florida, he went on to become a Green Beret and the intelligence officer for the 6th Special Forces Group in Fort Bragg, North Carolina. (BT.)

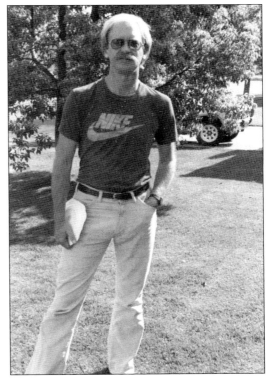

Bob Tribe is shown around 1979. After leaving the service, he returned to Sacramento and went to work for the State of California. From 1975 to 2000, Tribe was an administrator for the Fair Political Practices Commission, serving as the agency's executive director for the last five. In retirement, Tribe has led hikes through the Sierra Nevada Mountains and volunteered as an oral historian at the Sacramento Public Library. (BT.)

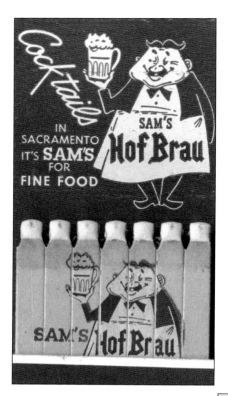

Shown is a promotional matchbook for the beloved Sacramento institution Sam's Hof Brau. Restaurateur Sam Gordon opened up his first location at Seventeenth and J Streets in 1955, growing his empire into 11 eateries, including 6 in the Sacramento area. Gilded heat lamps, carved roast beef, pastrami, turkey, and corned beef sandwiches; free pickles; red velveteen wallpaper; and wood paneling were signature features of the cafeteria-style restaurants.

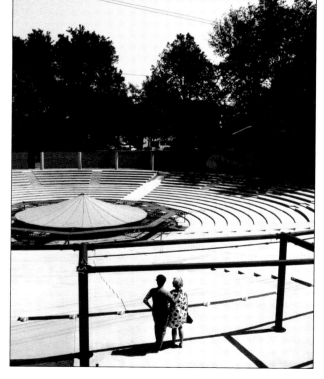

Starting in 1951, the Sacramento theater community would never be the same as Music Circus put down stakes at Fifteenth and H Streets, offering an annual 10-week stand of summertime musical theater. Tied into Music Circus lore are impromptu visits from Gov. Pat Brown, who, dressed in swimsuit and robe, would peak in for a quick dose of theater after swimming in the pool of the adjacent Mansion House Inn.

Sacramento attorney and civil rights champion Nathaniel Colley is shown in 1950. The Alabama-born, Yale-educated Colley was a self-described "country lawyer" who became so much more than that in fighting both local and nationwide discriminatory practices in housing, education, and employment. Colley also served on Pres. John F. Kennedy's Committee on Equal Opportunity in the Armed Forces. (BL.)

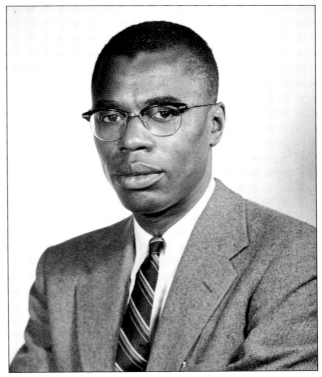

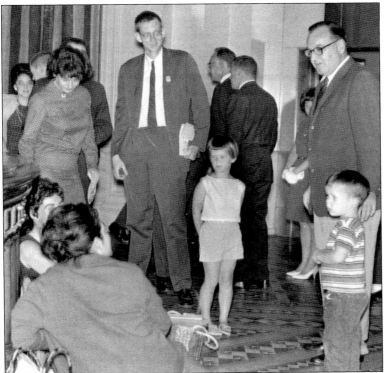

In 1963, Congress of Racial Equality members protest within the capitol to support the Rumford Fair Housing Act, which outlawed racial discrimination in housing accommodations. Gov. Pat Brown (far right) and his grandchildren Kathleen and Joey engage protestors, who used signage and singing to make their point. Of the protestors, Brown told his grandchildren, "It is perfectly all right for them . . . we all have our own ways of achieving our objectives."

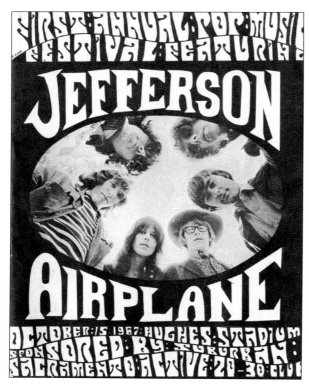

Jefferson Airplane played Hughes Stadium on October 15, 1967, as the headliner of the Sacramento Pop Music Festival. Attendees, who saw notables like the Nitty Gritty Dirt Band, Strawberry Alarm Clock, and Sacramento's own The Breed, also enjoyed a surprise performance from Captain Beefheart and His Magic Band, who played several songs from their new album, *Safe as Milk*.

US Marine sergeant Michael Hodgson, a graduate of Fair Oaks' Bella Vista High School, was stationed near the demilitarized zone between South and North Vietnam in 1966 and 1967. During his deployment, he expressed his Vietnam War experiences—everything from dysentery to combat—in "With Sgt. Mike," a series that started running in the *Sacramento Bee* and grew into nationwide syndication.

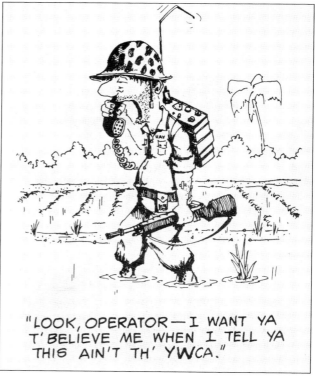

"LOOK, OPERATOR—I WANT YA T'BELIEVE ME WHEN I TELL YA THIS AIN'T TH' YWCA."

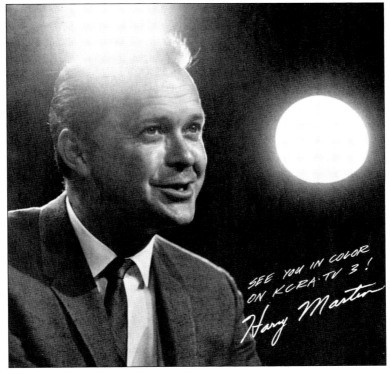

Shown above is a 1965 KCRA television logo, created to promote the station's commitment to transmitting its news segments in color. Hitting the airwaves on September 3, 1955, with a signal that reached as far north as Yuba City, south to Stockton, and west to Oakland, the station declared itself as the place "Where the News Comes First." The legendary Stan Atkinson lived those words with in-depth, on-location reports from hotspots like South Vietnam and Central America. Shown below is Harry Martin, one of the most beloved faces of Sacramento television, working for KCRA for nearly three decades from 1956 to 1989. Whether as "space volunteer" Captain Sacto with an assignment of "cartoon fun for everyone" or freewheeling wisecracker in a segment of Bob Wilkins's "Creature Features," Martin had a million-dollar smile and a gift for seamlessly connecting with viewers.

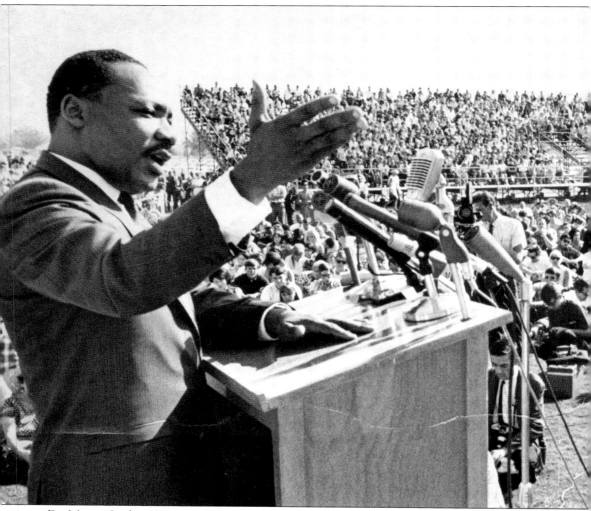

Dr. Martin Luther King Jr. addresses nearly 6,000 at Sacramento State College during the late morning of October 16, 1967. Speaking only weeks before announcing his intent to wage war on poverty with the Poor People's Campaign and just months after coming out against the Vietnam War, King reemphasized the value of nonviolence in promoting the cause of African Americans while also stressing the imperative of action, stating "progress never rolls in on the wheels of inevitability." By contrast, a year later and not five months after King's assassination, fiery Black

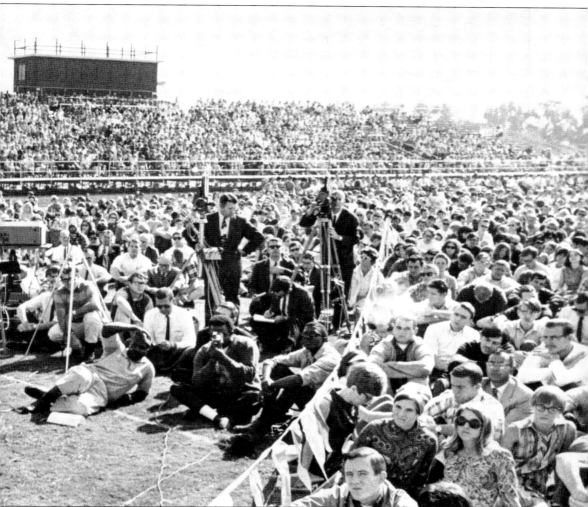

Panther Party leader Eldridge Cleaver addressed a crowd of 10,000, referring to the presidential race between Richard Nixon, Hubert Humphrey, and George Wallace as "a choice between oink, oink, and oink," while demanding the nationalization of phone and power utilities. Many were stunned by Cleaver's rhetoric, but a young history professor named Gregg Campbell expressed that, "although a painful and shattering experience" for many, "it had a salutary shock value in forcing white liberals to examine their own hypocrisies and neat expectations." (CSH.)

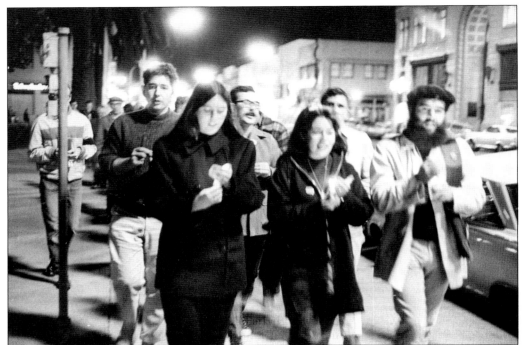

Mourners round City Plaza at Tenth and J Streets on the evening of April 4, 1968, in response to the assassination of Dr. Martin Luther King Jr. Labor leader Cesar Chavez joined the candlelight vigil, which featured freedom songs and a rendition of the La Huelga anthem, "De Colores." By day's end, the city council had named the new public library at Twenty-Fourth Street and Florin Road after King. (CSH.)

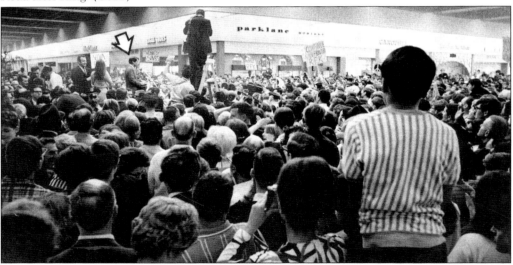

An arrow indicates a campaigning Robert F. Kennedy at Florin Center in March 1968. An estimated 14,000 citizens listened to the US senator claim that "decency is at the heart of this [presidential primary] campaign . . . poverty is indecent . . . the death and maiming of brave young men in the jungles and swamps of Southeast Asia is also indecent." Within months, Kennedy would be dead, felled by an assassin's bullet in Los Angeles. (CSH.)

At right, members of Oak Park's chapter of the Black Panther Party occupy Sacramento City Council chambers in an effort to protest police actions during the so-called Father's Day Riot of June 16, 1969. Oak Park, home to most of the city's nearly 18,000 African American residents, was consumed with violence after a massive police response was launched against the Black Panther headquarters at 2941 Thirty-Fifth Street, the supposed origin of gunshots. A subsequent police raid on the headquarters, which was empty, did enough damage to shut down the Panther's children's free breakfast program for nearly a week. Below, police crouch behind a squad car during the riots. Of the nearly 20 people injured over the six-hour melee, three were hospitalized, including *Sacramento Union* reporter Hoyt Elkins, who suffered stab wounds to the head and chest. (Both, CSH.)

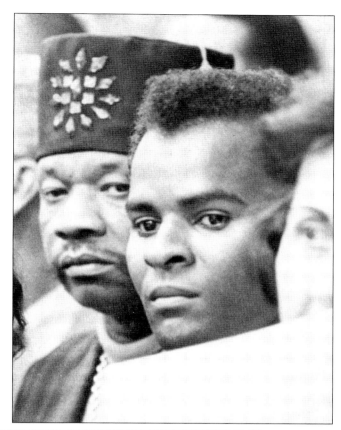

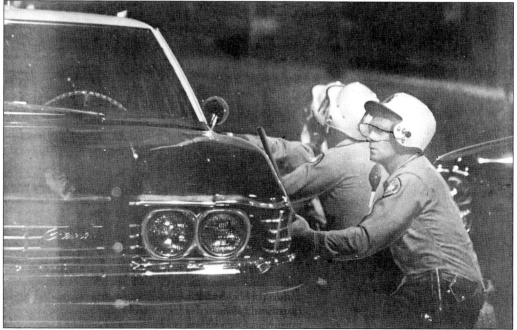

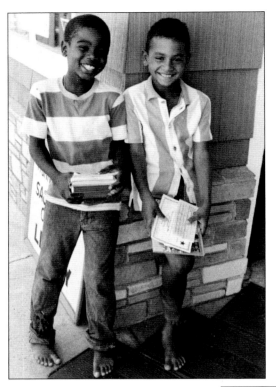

Boys smile in the summer of 1968 with books in hand just outside the Fruitridge branch of the Sacramento County Library. They represent the changing face of Sacramento. Nonwhite, non-Hispanic Sacramentans made up 10 percent of the population in 1970, then 20 percent in 1980, and 25 percent in 1990. By 2002, Sacramento—comprised of 59 percent nonwhites—was called the most diverse city in the United States by *Time* magazine.

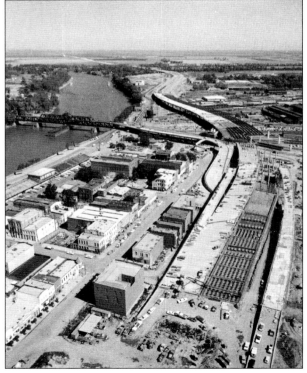

The placement of Interstate 5 pitted historic preservationists against the business community and city in what late city historian James Henley called "the greatest controversy to hit the city in the last half of the twentieth-century." *Sacramento Bee* editor and preservationist Eleanor McClatchy begged Pres. John F. Kennedy to intercede. He did, ensuring that the road's path bent around the Old Sacramento National Historic Landmark, as pictured in May 1968. (CSH.)

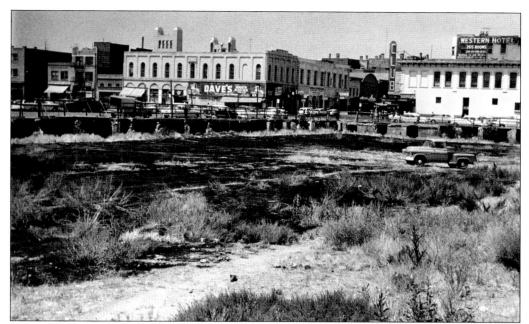

Shown in 1960 is the instant impact of redevelopment between J and K Streets and Third and Fourth Streets. Slated to be a Macy's parking lot, it was just 20 years earlier that the block was a multiethnic, multiracial community with surnames like Fong, Puccinelli, Diaz, and Miyasaki. Also revealed were remnants of primeval Sacramento, hidden away with the raising of the city's streets in 1863 to avoid flooding.

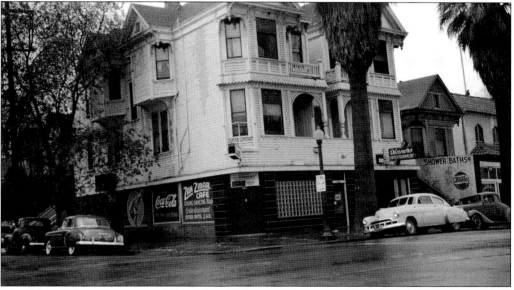

The African American–owned Zan Zibar Club sits at the corner of Sixth and M Streets in April 1950. The Zan Zibar was an artistic hub that, while hosting jazz greats like Duke Ellington and Louis Armstrong, was also an early conductor of cross-cultural integration. A revolving stage, Egyptian-style wall hangings, mint juleps, and Southern-style fried chicken accented the Zan Zibar's interior. Postwar redevelopment eliminated the club's presence and much of its history. (CSH.)

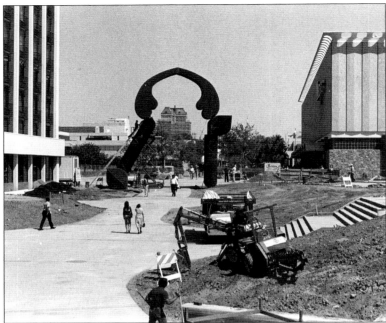

Shown in April 1980 at Third and K Streets is the 40-foot-high "Indo Arch." Designed by Sacramento State art professor Gerald Walburg amid controversy, it was the result of the city council's decision to spend two percent of the redevelopment budget on public art. The Holiday Inn sits to the left and Macy's is to the right, with the 926 J Street building positioned within the graceful curves of the arch.

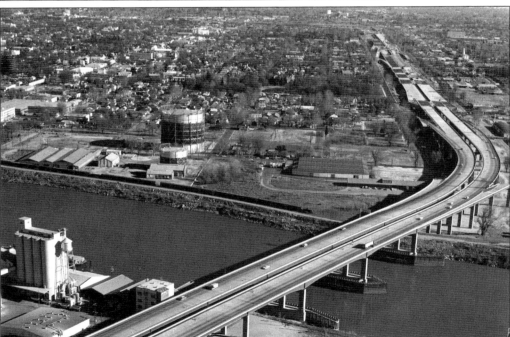

By the late 1950s, Sacramento was considered one of the most difficult California cities to drive through, with one journalist calling it "a monstrous, smog-belching serpent." With bridges and freeways considered solutions, a newish Pioneer Memorial Bridge feeds the W-to-X Street Freeway in 1967. Although the westernmost portion of the viaduct is open, drivers waited another year for the Fifteenth-to-Thirtieth Street section to be connected to the Twenty-Ninth-to-Thirtieth Street Freeway. (CSH.)

A fountain and so-called "tank trap" sit at the intersection of Eleventh and K Streets in 1974. The redesign closed K Street to vehicular traffic, populating the avenue in the 1960s and 1970s with a seven-block combination of sculptures, fountains, and rushing water in an effort to revitalize what had been Sacramento's commercial heart. By 1983, the universally maligned structures were removed, making room for the new light-rail system.

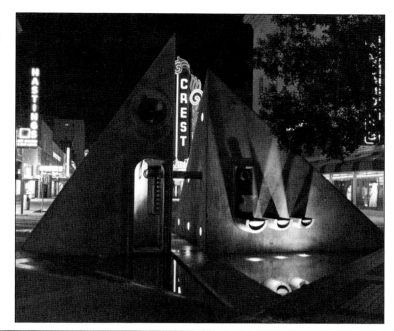

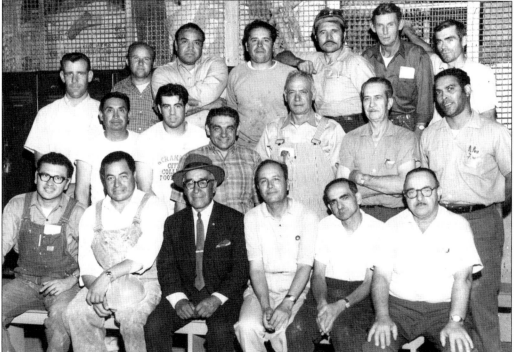

Painters at Sacramento's Southern Pacific (SP) Railroad shops pose for this 1969 photograph. As of 1969, SP had 4,500 workers at both its Sacramento and Roseville shops, carrying forth the well-earned tradition of being the region's highest profile and longest operating mechanized industry. SP's purchase by Union Pacific in 1996–1998 effectively closed the shops. As of 2019, the roughly 250-acre reservation is undergoing environmental remediation with an eye to repurposing.

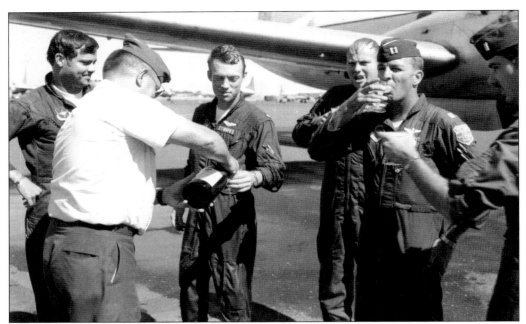

At the end of 78 days of training, navigator-bombardier graduates sip champagne just outside a T-29 "Flying Classroom" at Mather Air Force Base in 1972. Beyond national defense, the economic impact of both Mather and McClellan was undeniable. For the 1971–1972 fiscal year, the bases generated more than $27 million in county tax receipts, while taxable sales to both military and civilian employees amounted to $227 million.

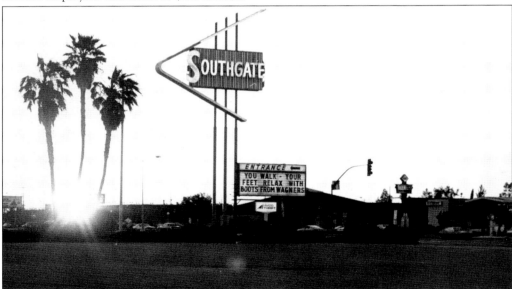

This 1975 photograph captures the California sun setting behind a triad of palms and signage for the Southgate shopping center at Franklin Boulevard and Florin Road, which opened in 1960. By 1966, Southgate and four other suburban shopping centers, Arden Fair, Town & Country, Country Club, and Cordova Village, were out-earning Sacramento's downtown retail core by nearly $12 million—a clear sign of changing times.

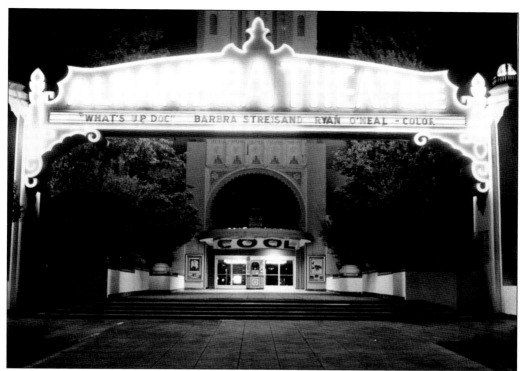

The neon shines bright for Streisand and O'Neal, and the air-conditioning operates on full blast at the venerable Alhambra Theatre in the spring of 1972. Opening in 1927, it was at the plush, Moorish-style venue that couples fell in love, children saw their first film, and all worries were cast away. The theater stood sentinel over Alhambra Boulevard until its demolition in 1973.

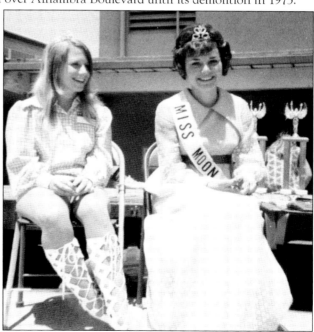

This 1972 photograph shows newly crowned Moonwalk Festival "Miss Moon" Michele Schultz (right). The Moonwalk Festival started in North Highlands in July 1970 to commemorate the Apollo 11 moon landing and subsequent moonwalk by Neil Armstrong. It offered a parade (one year with nearly 150 floats), music, a talent show, and celebrities, including *Star Trek*'s George Takei and a Playboy centerfold. The festival was last held in 1984.

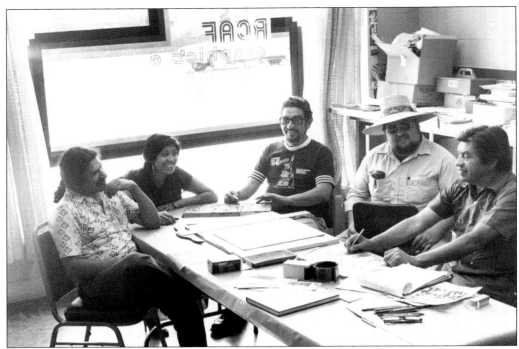

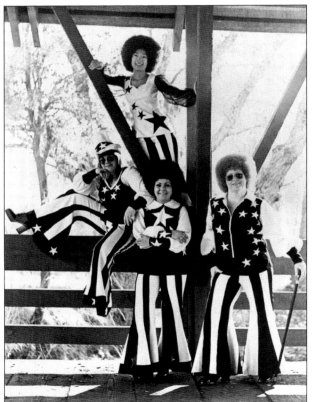

This c. 1980 image shows members of the Royal Chicano Air Force at the group's graphics and design center. From left to right are Juanishi Orosco, unidentified, José Montoya, Ricardo Favela, and Esteban Villa. The Alkali Flat–based group, known officially as the Rebel Chicano Art Front, was the artistic and marketing arm of the Chicano liberation movement of the 1960s, 1970s, and 1980s. (CSH.)

Pictured in 1972 is the Sacramento-based rock group Thundermama. Signed under the Marina Records label, the all-female ensemble were, from left to right, double-neck guitarist Leigh Montgomery, drummer Gayle Lee, lead singer Deane Calvin, and organist, pianist, and accordion player Renee Ella. The group played a diverse array of Sacramento venues, including Mather Field, Watt Avenue's Candlerock, and the California State Fair.

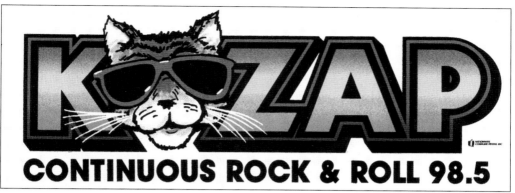

CONTINUOUS ROCK & ROLL 98.5

KZAP, Sacramento's fabled free-form radio station, was launched atop the Elks Tower in 1968. Bucking the industry standard to play only mainstream sets, KZAP was unique, letting DJs go their own way with eclectic rock playlists and lesser-known cuts from albums of the day. The station reached its ratings peak in the 1980s, but eventually changed its format to country in 1992. Shown is KZAP's signature orange cat.

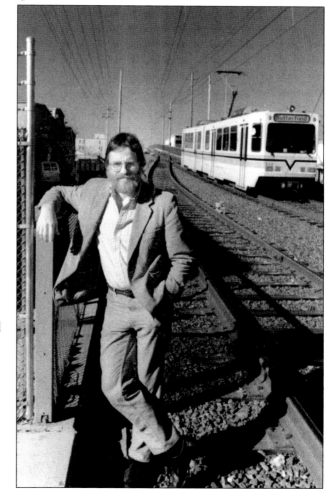

Shown in December 1989 is light-rail activist Tom Whitney, founder of Light Rail and Transit Advocates. The group spearheaded two tax measures that became essential in expanding light-rail service. Whitney also promoted "pedestrian pockets," a reversion to turn-of-the-century England's "railroad suburbs" as a way to encourage walking. One such spot, University City, was to house up to 5,000 people and be located near Power Inn Road and Highway 50. (CSH.)

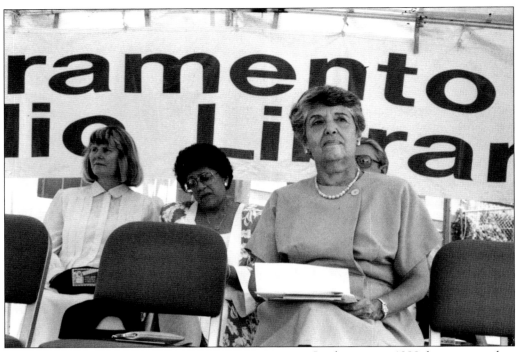

Looking on in 1988 during ground-breaking ceremonies for the new Sacramento Public Library Central Branch is Anne Rudin, the first woman to be elected mayor of Sacramento. She held the post from 1983 to 1992, during which time she oversaw the implementation of light rail, pushed through ordinances for cleaner air, helped smooth the closure and repurposing of the area's military bases, and acted as a tireless advocate for the arts.

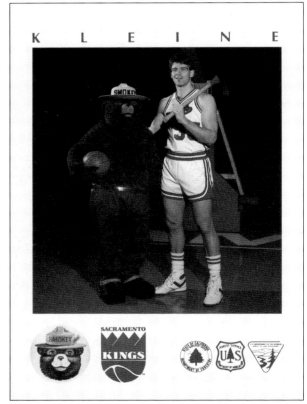

Posing with Smokey Bear in 1985 is the Sacramento Kings' very first draft choice, Joe Kleine. While the Kings did much to change Sacramento's sporting culture, the gentle giant did little to change the Kings. The high-water season for the club came in 2001–2002 with a 61-21 record and playoff run that ended with a bitterly controversial loss to the Los Angeles Lakers in the Western Conference finals.

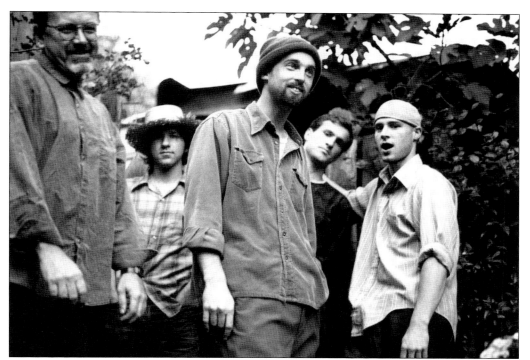

Shown in 1992 is the Sacramento-based alternative music group Cake. The band rose to nationwide fame in the late 1990s and early 2000s, boasting a signature sound that incorporated eclectic genres, clever lyrics, and monotone vocals. From left to right are guitarist Greg Brown, singer and guitarist John McCrea, trumpeter Vince Difiore, and bassist Gabe Nelson. Drummer Frank French is not pictured. (CSH.)

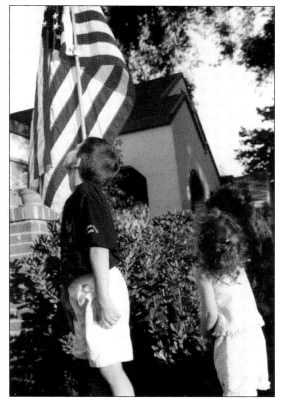

The attacks of September 11, 2001, sent Sacramento into a prolonged state of shock. The legislative office building was evacuated, passengers readying for takeoff at the Sacramento International Airport were deplaned, and area Arab and Muslim leaders quickly condemned the incident that claimed the lives of nearly 3,000 citizens. In the front yard of their Woodlake home, two children show their patriotism on the attack's first anniversary. (Kristy Molnar.)

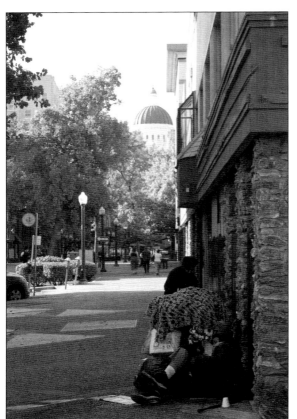

As with the 1848 squatters' riots and the Great Depression's Hoovervilles, generations of Sacramentans have known the sting of homelessness. In the summer of 2018, homeless citizens sit just below the splendor of the California State Capitol dome at Cathedral Square at Eleventh and K Streets. In 2017, the homelessness issue became critical as a countywide census counted 3,665 homeless, an increase of 30 percent from 2015.

Demonstrators representing Black Lives Matter make their way through the intersection of Eighth and J Streets in September 2018 in an effort to protest a peace officers' convention at the Sacramento Convention Center. Just six months earlier, unarmed, 22-year-old African American Stephon Clark was killed by Sacramento Police, stoking already heated tensions between law enforcement and protestors in the Sacramento region and around the nation.

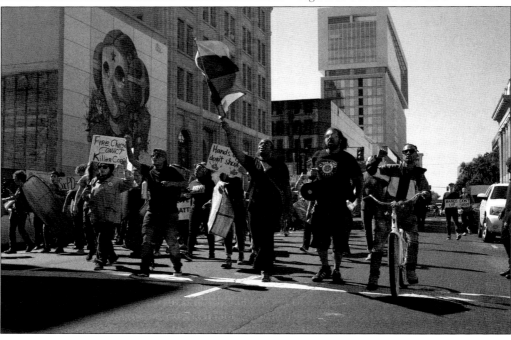

It is through Wide Open Walls, an annual art festival attracting muralists from both near and far, that artistic expression is brought to the everyday lives of Sacramentans in the hopes of engendering a sense of civic pride. Several festival creations, including Maren Conrad's "Lady Bird" (right) and activist Shepard Fairey's "Johnny Cash" (below) speak to the capital region's plucky drive toward the future as well as its full-hearted embrace of a gritty past. *Lady Bird*, an optimistic story about a precocious teen and so-called "love letter to Sacramento" expertly scribed by Sacramento-born director Greta Gerwig, was nominated for five Academy Awards. The 15-story-high Cash mural looks east from the corner of Sixteenth and L Streets. As a champion of prisoner rehabilitation and promoter of incarceration reform, Cash played two shows to prisoners at Folsom State Prison in January 1968.

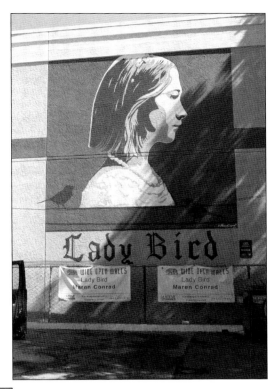

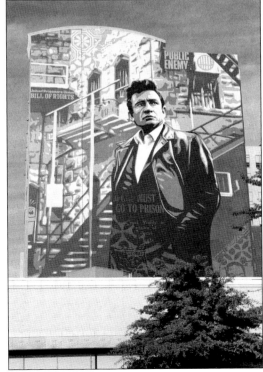

Discover Thousands of Local History Books
Featuring Millions of Vintage Images

Arcadia Publishing, the leading local history publisher in the United States, is committed to making history accessible and meaningful through publishing books that celebrate and preserve the heritage of America's people and places.

Find more books like this at
www.arcadiapublishing.com

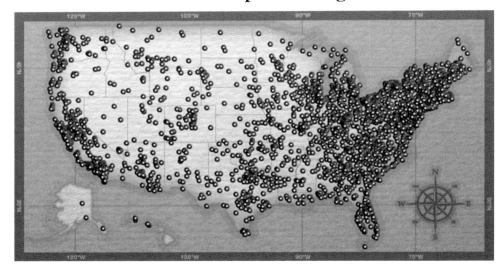

Search for your hometown history, your old stomping grounds, and even your favorite sports team.

Consistent with our mission to preserve history on a local level, this book was printed in South Carolina on American-made paper and manufactured entirely in the United States. Products carrying the accredited Forest Stewardship Council (FSC) label are printed on 100 percent FSC-certified paper.

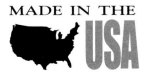

MADE IN THE USA